Volume Two

Favorite Bible Passages

More Lessons From Familiar Texts

Contents

A New Look at
Time-tested Words

On a warm July Sunday the pastor announced the opening hymn. The organist began to play familiar sounds, but people looked at one another with puzzled or amused expressions. Somewhat hesitantly the congregation sang,

> Joy to the world,
> the Lord is come!
> Let earth receive her king. [1]

The words seemed out of place. The wrong time of year! Then the pastor explained that this hymn, based on Psalm 98, contained nothing in its message that limited its use to December. We can proclaim all year long that the Lord has come and rules our world with truth and grace.

Sometimes it takes a jolt to make us look at familiar words in a fresh way. This study of FAVORITE BIBLE PASSAGES rests on a belief that God uses the familiar to bring us new understanding and insight.

When you were half your present age, some of the Bible's messages may have meant much to you or nothing at all. The meaning won't be the same today. The living God who speaks through the Scriptures offers new meanings for new situations.

Not all these readings will be equally familiar, but all are the kind that Christians have turned to again and again across the generations.

If you have a favorite Bible passage that we have failed to include, we will be pleased for you to let us know.

The Editors
Favorite Bible Passages
201 Eighth Avenue, South,
P.O. Box 801
Nashville, TN 37202

---

[1]From "Joy to the World," *The United Methodist Hymnal* (Copyright © 1989 The United Methodist Publishing House); No. 246.

3

Finding Christ Through the Bible

By Brady B. Whitehead, Jr.

One of the most valuable lessons I ever learned about studying the Bible came from a kindly man in his late seventies. He thought he was complimenting me on a job well done. What he did not know at the time, though I told him later, was that his remark deeply disturbed me. His words caused me to change my whole approach to leading Bible study groups in the church. Mr. Lewis made that remark more than thirty years ago, but I remember it as though it were yesterday.

I had finished seminary and was working on a graduate degree in Biblical Studies. The church where I was the associate pastor asked me to lead the congregation in a survey of the Old Testament. I agreed to do so, and we set aside eight Sunday nights for that purpose. At the conclusion of the third week of the study, Mr. Lewis made his remark. That session had brought us to the death of Solomon. I announced that the following week we would look at the revolution that erupted after Solomon's death and at the civil war that cut the nation of Israel in two. As the people were leaving that night, there was the usual round of hand shaking and commenting on the study. Mr. Lewis was one of the people who shook my hand. "I like the way you teach the Bible," he said. Had he said no more than that, his words would have had no significant impact on my life. However, he went on to explain what he meant: "You teach the Bible as history and not as a lot of God stuff."

To say that I was stunned by his words would be an understatement. Was I really being so unfaithful to the message of the Bible that I was teaching it as merely history and not as "God stuff?" *Surely not*, I thought. Yet Mr. Lewis's words haunted me. Over the next few days I found myself reviewing over and over all the things that I had said in the first three sessions of the study. Before the next Sunday night had arrived, I had made both a confession and a vow. My confession was that there was more truth in Mr. Lewis's words than I cared to admit. My vow was that never again would I teach the history of Israel as though it were nothing more than human history. The plain teaching of the Scriptures is that God was the primary actor in that history. I promised that I would make sure that from then on that fact would come through in my teaching.

Perhaps this experience was what caused me to be overjoyed to learn of an increased emphasis in the church school on invitational teaching. For that experience of many years ago took me beyond just the issue raised that night and led me ultimately to an invitational approach to the Scriptures. I realized that not only is God the primary actor in the history of Israel, God is also the primary actor in our history and in our lives today. Just as God spoke to the people of Israel through the written word then, so also does God speak to us through the Scriptures now. The Bible constantly invites us to come to Christ, not just to hear what he said to the people of his own day but also to commit ourselves to him as we hear him calling to us. That fact is at the very heart of what it means to call the books of the Bible "Scripture."

How does having such an understanding affect the way we study the Bible? Having such an understanding means that we approach the Scriptures in an attitude of expectancy, of listening to hear what God has to say to us. Having such an understanding means that our concern is not just to learn what Jesus or Paul or Moses did long ago but also to learn what God would have us do in the present. One way to do this, a way that I have found helpful, is to ask a series of questions. The first question I ask is, "What did this passage mean to the person who wrote it and to those who first read it?" We can discover this meaning through the use of good commentaries and through the many teaching and learning helps made available by the church. We need to begin with this question because not every thought that comes to mind as we read the Scriptures is from God. We can come away from our study with the wrong interpretation of the passage. We minimize this possibility, however, if we have an understanding of the original meaning of the passage. For though the message God has for us today may be an extension of the original message of the passage, it will never be a contradiction of it.

Our exploration of the passage must not stop there, however. I had made that mistake when I was a young associate pastor. I had ferreted out the historical truths for the congregation, but I had failed to go on to ask the invitational questions. Failing to do so always gives only a partial hearing of the Scriptures, for the Bible really is "God stuff." Through its pages God calls to us, and our study of the Bible is never complete until we hear and answer that call. We must ask, "What word from the Lord does this passage have for me now in the situations that I face in the 1990's—in my church, in my place of employment, in my home, and in my neighborhood?" We seek to discover, "How is my life similar to the situation depicted in this passage? How is it different? How much of this passage speaks immediately and directly to my situation? How might God extend the message of old to cover other aspects of my present situation?" And most important, "What invitation does God have for me today? Is there something God would have me to do, something God would have me to say, some particular way God is calling on me to live? Just what is God's invitation to me today?" When we attempt to answer such questions, the Bible truly becomes God's word for us. I shall be forever grateful to Mr. Lewis for helping me to understand that fact.

The Scripture lessons in this second volume of FAVORITE BIBLE PASSAGES quite likely are all familiar to us. We have probably read them many times and probably know the historical significance of most of them. However, we may have never heard them as God's personal invitation to us. If not, we need to read them afresh; for there is a lot of "God stuff" in these passages. God is waiting for us to listen, to hear, and to respond.

Dr. Whitehead is a professor of religion at Lambuth College, Jackson, Tennessee.

1

Adam and Eve
Genesis 2:4–3:24

The Lord God commanded the man, saying, "You may freely eat of every tree of the garden; but of the tree of the knowledge of good and evil you shall not eat, for in the day that you eat of it you shall die."

Genesis 2:16-17

WORDS FOR BIBLE TIMES

Adam and Eve are not mentioned in the first chapter of Genesis. That account of Creation is seen through a wide-angle lens, looking at the whole earth, the whole sky, the whole universe. Genesis 2, beginning with verse 4, takes a different approach. This account shows us that God was actively involved in the details of Creation. To make a human being, God gathered the dust, shaped the figure, then blew God's own breath into its nostrils. Next God made a garden for the human. In the garden was all that person needed: food, shade, beauty, a task, and finally another human. The two, male and female, were the crowning achievement of Creation. Then God set limits to protect this pair, Adam and Eve. One piece of God's creation would be dangerous for Adam and Eve. They were not to touch the tree at the center of the garden.

To help us understand what this passage of Scripture is saying, we first need to understand what it is not saying. We do not find here a story to explain how evil came into the world. This passage of Scripture is not a story to explain why women have pain in childbirth or why work can become a drudgery. It is most certainly not a story about the possible evils brought about by sex.

The temptation in the garden had to do with knowledge as a form of power. What Adam and Eve forgot was that God was the powerful partner in the relationship. In taking the fruit, Adam and Eve tried to create new limits instead of accepting those God established. The consequence of their decision to live outside God's limits was death (Genesis 2:17).

The consequence, death, appeared to be non-negotiable. However, God's love for God's people reduced the penalty of immediate death to one of leaving the perfect garden for an imperfect world. While this part of the account has often been seen as a punishment, it needs also to be seen as a statement about God's love and God's grace. God's severe wrath is secondary to God's extension of new opportunities to sinful persons.

WORDS FOR OUR TIME

Independence has become an important word in our society. We have taught children that they must be able to work, think, and act independently. We tell married couples that it is a healthy pattern to stay somewhat independent of each other. Individuals should not always depend on their spouses to act for them or to think for them.

While all these words of advice are true and important, too much stress on independence puts us at risk of forgetting our dependence on God. The challenge for us today is to teach our children, and truly to realize ourselves, that we can depend on God without losing our integrity and our responsibility for our actions.

Ironically, in a time when we seek to foster independence in school, home, and workplace, we seem less and less willing to take responsibility for our actions. Elected officials pass on to others the responsibility for a bad decision or simply deny knowledge of the event. Upper-management personnel blame their corporation's poor performance on lower-level personnel who in turn blame it on the plant workers who pass it back to their immediate superiors in the same way that Adam blamed Eve, and Eve blamed the serpent.

Our society has made it easier each year for people to function independently of one another. In our homes two persons are no longer necessary to do the dishes, one to wash and one to dry. And while American families have hung up the dishtowel with glee, they have also lost a natural time of conversation and growth as a household. Forming relationships and keeping them in repair has become more difficult because we can easily do by ourselves tasks that once required two or more people. Appliances can perform a greater part of any task than ever before. At their best these devices should allow us more time with our families and friends. But in many cases they simply allow us to move to our solitary activities more quickly and with less interference.

God's people were always intended to be in relationship with God and with others. Every relationship is made possible by God's relationship with us. Our relationships with friends, coworkers, children, and spouse are influenced by our relationship with God.

WORDS FOR MY LIFE

Genesis 3:8-10 portrays Adam and Eve as being very frightened. Each of us can probably remember "getting caught" as a child, whether it was for passing a note at school or for breaking the heirloom in the living room where we were not supposed to have been running. Remember for a moment that anxiety, that fear. At the moment of getting caught and even more in the long agonizing moments afterward, waiting for punishment, we were not completely confident about how much our parents or teacher loved and cared about us. Our fear cancelled out our full understanding of love.

Each of us is bombarded daily with things that others

say should make us fearful. The media tell us we should fear the loss of our looks, our health, our financial security, and our youth. What are your fears? How much money will you spend to pursue the myth that we must all look young to be happy? How much time will you spend climbing the corporate ladder while you lose opportunities to develop deeper relationships with your family and friends?

Life would have been simpler if there had been no troublesome tree at the center of the garden. Then we would not have to make so many choices. But there is a tree. In our own lives we all have a tree, maybe more than one, that tempts us. Consider your tree. Then decide how you can stay in relationship with God and still live with the tree in your garden.

2

The Flood
Genesis 6–9

God said, "This is the sign of the covenant which I make between me and you and every living creature that is with you, for all future generations: I set my bow in the cloud, and it shall be a sign of the covenant between me and the earth."

Genesis 9:12-13

WORDS FOR BIBLE TIMES

God is saddened, grieved to his heart (Genesis 6:6), as the story opens. All that God had imagined for creation had been skewed the wrong way. The creation that God had pronounced "good" had become evil. That evil was not within the waters, plants, or birds, however. The evil was dwelling within people, in the "imagination of the thoughts of [their] heart" (Genesis 6:5).

The story of the Flood existed in oral form before it was written down in the version we now have. Other accounts of a world-destroying flood are found in the writings of other early civilizations, both in the Middle East and across the globe.

This incident showed the early Israelites that God had definite expectations for humankind. But human beings did not live up to those expectations. So God made plans to destroy creation and to start again rather than allow the violence and lawlessness to continue. Standing opposite this violent world was Noah, who was righteous, blameless, and who walked with God. As a result, God decided to preserve a remnant. Noah and his family were saved in the ark. The Bible does not say that Noah's wife, sons, and sons' wives were righteous. Perhaps Noah's righteousness sufficed for all of them.

The Flood was catastrophic. All creatures were destroyed except for those with Noah in the ark.

About five months passed with water covering everything (Genesis 7:24). The passengers on the ark must have had times of despair as they looked toward the horizon. Then "God remembered Noah" (Genesis 8:1). Because God remembered Noah, God caused the waters to subside. Throughout history God's people often have wondered if God remembered them in their pain, just as we wonder now. Those who first heard or read this account of the Flood found assurance that God did not forget God's people.

After the Flood, Noah built an altar and made sacrifices on it (Genesis 8:20). God found the smell of the burnt offerings pleasing. Ritual obedience to the laws of worship and sacrifice pleased God. God's comment after the sacrifice (Genesis 8:21-22) may make us wonder what had been accomplished. Humankind was still evil at heart, but God accepted that as the way creation turned out. God made a move of righteous love and gracious redemption. God promised never to destroy the whole world by a flood again, guaranteeing the continuing cycle of the seasons. The people of early Israel, who depended heavily on rains not only for the growth of their crops but also for the continued natural vegetation to feed their herds, understood that their existence depended on the unchanging cycle of the seasons. Again the story of Noah brought reassurance.

WORDS FOR OUR TIME

We cannot read this passage without considering what God's feelings are about humankind today in terms of the evil imaginations of our hearts. The words of judgment are difficult to hear, but the words of grace fill us with hope. We pick up the newspaper daily to find yet more actions that deserve God's disappointment, anger, and judgment. The chaos before the Flood could have been no greater than the chaos of our world. Our very existence is threatened by stockpiles of nuclear weapons that could destroy the earth many times over. Is this the generation that should be wiped out? Is our world the one that should be washed clean so God can start everything again?

Our task as Christians is to be the Noahs of our day. We are to be the righteous who are blameless and who walk with God. Notice that Noah is not shown speaking God's words; he was not a prophet. Rather, Noah lived his righteousness. He knew that right living, that is, being faithful to God in business practices, in family relationships, in friendships, and in worship and sacrifice, is what God expects of humankind. God's people are to be models of faithfulness. We are known by what we do more than by what we say. If we live faithfully in every area of our lives, we will come closer to fulfilling God's expectations of us than if we only act out that faithfulness by our participation in church activities.

The end of this account of the Flood is the marvelous image of God placing God's bow in the sky (Genesis 9:11-13). A bow is a weapon. This instrument of death is put to rest and laid aside as a reminder that never again will creation drive God to the point of picking up his bow to destroy the earth. Our whole approach to life can be one that is free of fear and punishment because we are the children of the God who made a promise, a covenant, never to destroy us.

WORDS FOR MY LIFE

If we can imagine ourselves in Noah's place as the ark floated through 40 days of rain and another 150 days of unabating water, we may begin to understand what it means to have a fear of abandonment. Noah had hinged his whole faith on the belief that God would not forget him, his family, and the animals in the ark. Noah came through a time of chaos and destruction more violent than anything he had ever seen before and found the newness of God's promise symbolized by the hope-filled rainbow.

We all have our times of deep water. We may have to face the loss of a job, a rocky marriage, or a child who causes us a great deal of disappointment. We may have to deal with a serious physical illness or an emotional set-back. All or any of these situations can cause people to be filled with despair and a sense of loneliness. Many times we find ourselves wondering if God remembers us. We may even believe that when we suffer a loss—be it of health, job, financial security, or a precious relationship—we are being punished for something that we have done.

However, the good news, the grace, of the story of Noah is that God will not retaliate against creation again. God's heart has moved toward God's people. While many of our actions no doubt sadden and disappoint God, the Almighty is no longer waiting to retaliate. God's bow is at rest in the clouds. That weapon will not be taken up against God's people again. And that's a promise!

3

Jacob's Ladder
Genesis 28:10-22

Then Jacob awoke from his sleep and said, "Surely the LORD is in this place; and I did not know it."

Genesis 28:16

WORDS FOR BIBLE TIMES

This passage would not have been written except for the covenant God made with Jacob's grandfather Abraham. The promise God made to Abraham was that he would be blessed with land, riches, and children—all that he needed to be a powerful person in his day (Genesis 12:1-2). This blessing was given again to Abraham's son Isaac and was then to be passed on to Isaac's first-born son. Isaac and Rebekah had twin sons. Esau was the older son. But Jacob, whose name means trickster, had tricked his brother out of both his birthright and his blessing (Genesis 25:19-34). Our story picks up at the point where Jacob is on the run for his life. He and his mother, Rebekah, who had helped him steal the blessing, were afraid that Esau would try to kill him. So Jacob left home and went to live some distance away with his uncle Laban.

In this passage we find Jacob between safe locations. He had left the safety of home and was headed for the safety of his uncle's home. But this place, which is not even named until the end of the event, was not safe. Here Jacob was only a fugitive. Here Jacob had lost control. He was able to trick and scheme during his waking hours. But in dreams we are all vulnerable and out of control. Even the most powerful person on earth cannot control his or her dreams.

Into this vulnerable fugitive's life comes a *theophany*, a manifestation of God. Jacob sees a kind of ramp leading from heaven to earth. While the thought of climbing up to heaven may have fascinated Jacob, the idea that messengers of God could use the ramp to come to earth may have troubled him.

One value of this story for the Israelites rested in the kind of person Jacob was. He was not righteous, as was Abraham. He was not kind or morally upright. He was out for Number One, took whatever he could get, and tricked his family members out of anything he could. But God does not seem interested in moral fiber in this story. This story is about one of God's surprising choices—a choice that says God sees deeper or from a different perspective than humans.

The promises made in the covenant to Jacob go beyond that of land and descendants. This covenant promises that God will be with Jacob, protect him, and bring him back home in peace (Genesis 28:15). This story also said to the Israelites that there was hope for each of them. If God could choose Jacob to carry the covenant, then surely any one of the people of God could be set apart and used for God's purposes.

WORDS FOR OUR TIME

When Jacob awoke from his dream, he said, "Surely the LORD is in this place; and I did not know it" (Genesis 28:16). Jacob had come upon a sacred place. But notice that when Jacob pulled up a rock for a pillow to get some sleep, nothing about the place led Jacob to believe it was sacred (Genesis 28:11). In our society we tend to make certain places sacred because of how they look or because of certain people who are, or have been, in those places. But the reason this place was sacred to Jacob was because God's presence was there—and Jacob did not know it (at first).

We live in a world that is quite disturbing. The natural environment becomes more fragile every day. Families split apart, and the use of illegal drugs seems to be on the increase. Is it possible that God is in and among those things? Ask the young man dying in the AIDS ward where volunteers come to listen, read, and give support. Ask the child who is brought into a shelter and given food, warm clothes, and a bed. Ask the elderly woman in her boarded-up tenement when the free fans are brought in during the summer. Is God's presence there among the disease, the hunger, the roaches? Yes! Because this is a God who keeps promises. Situations may not always be changed; but a person's life can be changed by his or her realization that a sacred "place" can be any place, a place where God dwells. God once dwelt with Jacob in a "Godforsaken" wilderness when Jacob ran and hid from his justly angry brother. God dwells with us in those places we consider "Godforsaken," that is, frightening or evil. Sinful action can happen anywhere, but it happens in some places with greater frequency. If we realize that God is present in our lives, it will be easier to reach the presence of God in the life of another, anyplace. We become the stairway Jacob dreamed of that empowers God's message of love and grace and forgiveness to flow to humanity from God.

WORDS FOR MY LIFE

The earlier stories about Jacob and his family and those that follow this passage have to do with interaction between family members. Much of this interaction took the form of conflict. But in this passage no other family members are involved. The actions and words have to do with God and Jacob only. Do you need to find a time and place to be alone and vulnerable enough to hear and see God?

Jacob's message from God came in a dream. Perhaps that was because only in his dreams was Jacob open to God's Spirit. Jacob spent his waking hours trying to control his own destiny at every corner. Think about it.

Where in your life is a time and place to be open to God's presence? Are you so involved in making sure every part of your daily schedule is covered that you have forgotten to leave some time just to *be*? Would God need to come to you in a dream because you allow no time for God when you are awake?

Jacob is a fugitive from an angry brother. He stole his brother's birthright and blessing. How strange that in the heart of this far-from-perfect individual, God saw something that convinced God that Jacob should be the one to carry the covenant. In your own life is there something that makes it impossible for God to choose you for a special calling or work? If so, whose judgment is that? Who says so? Have you opened your heart and soul, imperfect though they are, to God's constantly abiding presence and power?

4

Joseph
Genesis 37–45; 50:15-21

As for you, you meant evil against me; but
God meant it for good, to bring it about that
many people should be kept alive, as they are
today.

Genesis 50:20

WORDS FOR BIBLE TIMES

Joseph, favorite son, beautiful coat: We know the story
well. Joseph was the son of Jacob by Rachel, his
favorite wife. Jacob's other sons pale in comparison to
Joseph. Joseph was a dreamer, perhaps not too bright
about human nature. In Genesis 37 we find the account of
how Joseph's brothers hated him because he was their
father's favorite. Nevertheless, Joseph seemed anxious to
tell his brothers about the dreams that showed him having
dominion over them. We shake our heads, wondering
about Joseph's lack of understanding in regard to his
brothers.

As a result of his brothers' actions, Joseph eventually
ended up as a slave in Egypt. He was unjustly accused of
having an affair with his owner's wife and was thrown in
jail. There Joseph used his ability to interpret dreams. The
plot moves quickly until we find Joseph standing in front
of Pharaoh, the ruler of all Egypt, listening to him
describe a disturbing dream. Joseph interpreted the dream,
and Pharaoh set him in a place of authority. There Joseph
was able to save the nation by collecting food during

seven years of plenty to distribute during seven years of famine.

Joseph's brothers and father were in need back home in the land of Canaan. The famine was severe there too. So the brothers came to Egypt, and Joseph met them. In some of the best writing in the Bible, we find ourselves swept along by the story. We know who Joseph is, and we know that his brothers do not recognize him. We know the cup is hidden in Benjamin's sack of grain, and we wait to see how the brothers will react. And at the end of Jacob's life, we wait to see how Joseph will respond.

This entire saga has a thread running through it that is missing from the other stories in Genesis. In this story it seems that there is no dramatic intervention from God; there is no emphasis on worship or altars. Instead, we find an ongoing understanding that God works within the natural events of our lives to bring God's promises and will to pass. The only appropriate response for human beings is to recognize that God is in all that happens.

This passage reminds us that some of our children are more lovable than others and that siblings will fight and sometimes be quite cruel to one another. We find here that righteousness pays off, even though it is in the distant future. We find that deep down inside, God's people always have the ability to forgive.

The story never explains itself. Instead, it twists and turns and finds God's will lurking just around each corner.

WORDS FOR OUR TIME

The story of Joseph brings to mind the constant tension people have between God's plan for their lives and their own free will. Did Joseph or his brothers have a choice about doing or not doing the things they did? Did God have it all planned, or did God work through the events of history to bring out goodness and righteousness in the end? When we raise that issue, we are really asking, "Does God work in and through the events in history that are shaping my own life? Is God's will able to be worked out through our government and through international politics? Does God set the course of history and pull us along as though we are riding with the tide?"

We find ourselves wondering how God can be at work amid terrorism, oppressive governments, possible nuclear destruction, and corruption in the offices we have set apart as deserving our respect. Yet the story of Joseph would have us realize that God is not a disinterested onlooker but an enabler of events in history. Trusting God means letting go of the control we think we have over certain events. "Letting go" does not mean we are to become irresponsible, however. Joseph kept his honor, his sense of justice and righteousness, when he was a servant in Potiphar's house, when he was in jail, and when he served as prime minister to Pharaoh. Perhaps such striving to live a righteous life is enough of an opening for God's will to be achieved.

Above all else as we observe our personal, national, and world situation, it is important to remember that we are God's people, bound to God by creation and covenant. God continues to care for creation, even when we abuse it. Although our actions may displease God intensely, God never stops caring about us. God is always there.

WORDS FOR MY LIFE

Throughout Joseph's time in Egypt, God was with him. We cannot say for sure that Joseph always felt God's presence. In fact, Joseph must have wondered often where God was, considering all the things that happened to him. Yet Joseph never stopped believing and trusting. Faith is believing that God is with us even when there seems to be no evidence of it.

Joseph was not promised, nor are we, that God would always make things good for him. But we can hold to the promise that God is with us. Joseph spent time in prison, and so do each of us, in prisons of our own making.

Even toward the end of this passage, we see that Joseph's brothers were afraid he would seek vengeance against them. Although Joseph had shown them every kindness up to this point, they still believe that perhaps his kindness was only because of Jacob. But now Jacob is dead, and Joseph holds all the cards. Yet Joseph forgives his brothers. In fact, not only does he forgive them, he sets his brothers free by absolving them of responsibility for what they did to him. Joseph does not pretend that their motives were good when they mistreated him. He just reminds them that their will was not as strong as God's will. God had found a way to use Joseph, to save not only his own people, but an entire nation.

Is something holding you back from forgiving someone who has wronged you, or even harder, from accepting forgiveness from someone you have wronged? Young Joseph may not have been sure of God's love, but the mature Joseph's love of God led him to his brothers as well as to God. When we really love, we really forgive. Only then can all the fear, guilt, and doubt be washed out of our lives.

5

The First Passover
Exodus 12:1-39

W hen your children say to you, "What do you mean by this service?" you shall say, "It is the sacrifice of the LORD's passover, for he passed over the houses of the people of Israel in Egypt, when he slew the Egyptians but spared our houses."

Exodus 12:26-27

WORDS FOR BIBLE TIMES

P ivotal to the Old Testament record, the Jewish understanding of God's action and presence with God's people, is the story of the Passover and the Exodus. To understand the Exodus, we must go back to Exodus 2:23-25. Here we find a concise description of the relationship between God and God's people: "In the course of those many days the king of Egypt died. And the people of Israel groaned under their bondage, and cried out for help, and their cry under bondage came up to God. And God heard their groaning, and God remembered his covenant with Abraham, with Isaac, and with Jacob. And God saw the people of Israel, and God knew their condition." The verbs *heard, remembered, saw,* and *knew* set the stage for God's response in Exodus 3:8: "I have come down to deliver them out of the hand of the Egyptians."

The relationship of God to the Israelites was one in which God understood all that was happening and then did something about it. God would not allow God's people to be oppressed any longer. God called Moses and sent him to Pharaoh. God caused the plagues to prove to Pharaoh just who was in charge and why Pharaoh should let the Hebrew people go.

The final plague is the basis for the core of our passage. God told Moses that unless the blood of a lamb was put on the doorpost over each house, the first-born in that house would die. If the blood was on the doorpost, the Lord would "pass over" the house and harm no one.

The people of Israel reenacted the Passover each year by the killing of the lamb and by eating it along with the unleavened bread and the bitter herbs. The ritual was a reminder that God would never forsake God's chosen people. The Passover ritual reminded Israel that God had set apart a land for God's people, a land that would always be theirs. The understanding was that when any oppression they were experiencing became unbearable, God would not tolerate it any longer. At that point God would intervene and deliver them. Note that God "remembered" the covenant made with Abraham, Isaac, and Jacob. God had promised blessings, land, God's presence, and descendants. In the Exodus, God acted on that promise. Celebrating the ritual of Passover each year keeps the people of Israel from forgetting how God rescued their ancestors from slavery and gave them the Promised Land.

WORDS FOR OUR TIME

We too are a people of memory. One of the strengths of the Jewish heritage is a long memory of God's love and God's presence. This heritage is thousands of years old and has defined the identity of the Hebrew people generation after generation. Think about the governments in our world today that are oppressive and unjust. Many people groan under bondage and cry out for help. Which Third World country comes to mind? Imagine living in a country where you can be killed, or, at the very least, imprisoned, for speaking out against the government. Imagine a place where you are not allowed to hold a job or to walk into a grocery store because of the color of your skin.

Not only other nations, but our own country comes to mind. Think of the sixteen-year-old single mother who knows nothing but life in the ghetto. She cannot afford to work because she has only a sixth-grade education, and her pay at the fast food restaurant where she is qualified to work would be less than her welfare check.

What about the mother of three small children who is being abused by her husband? She has no family nearby. If she leaves her husband and gets a job, half of her paycheck will go for day care for the children. She has to choose between living in poverty and living in an abusive household.

How would God be defined to persons in such situations? This passage should carry a special meaning to such persons. God sees, hears, knows, and delivers. What an incredible promise!

WORDS FOR MY LIFE

In the reenactment of the Passover, the youngest child in the family asks the questions concerning why these actions are taking place. As each family member responds to the questions, all the children learn what happened to their people so many years ago. The children begin to understand that this story is their story. God has set them apart and has delivered them.

Most of us have family stories and traditions that have shaped how we live. The memories we have help determine how we will live the rest of our lives. Some families have their own special traditions for holidays, birthdays, or other special occasions. Those traditions are similar to the Passover for Jews. Each time we act out a particular tradition, we bring into our memories the other times we have done the same thing. Parents pass on to children those things that were special to them when they were growing up. One of the greatest gifts grandparents can give their grandchildren is passing on the stories and traditions that have set their family apart and have made them unique. This is particularly true of religious traditions, or at least of family celebrations that are centered around church. When holidays or family celebrations are combined with our life in the church, the memory that belongs to the child, as well as to the adult, is one that says there is great joy in sharing our immediate family with our church family. This memory also says that our family is grounded in a tradition that goes back before our grandparents and great-grandparents lived. Our heritage goes back to Moses and to the God who remembered Abraham, Isaac, and Jacob. We share the same roots as do our Jewish friends, roots that go back to the first Passover. We were grafted onto that family tree. If God remembered the covenant made with Abraham, Isaac, and Jacob, then surely God will remember us.

6

The Benediction
Numbers 6:22-27

The LORD said to Moses, "Say to Aaron and his sons, Thus you shall bless the people of Israel: you shall say to them,

The LORD bless you and keep you:

The LORD make his face to shine upon you, and be gracious to you:

The LORD lift up his countenance upon you, and give you peace.

"So shall they put my name upon the people of Israel, and I will bless them."

Numbers 6:22-27

WORDS FOR BIBLE TIMES

The Book of Numbers is a sometimes interesting and sometimes boring look at the life of the Israelites after the giving of the Ten Commandments. This book describes their wanderings in the wilderness and their life as a community as they approached the Promised Land. In the Book of Numbers we have statistics and facts, laws and expectations. We see Moses becoming much more "human"; that is, we see his compassion as well as his faults. We learn how the Tabernacle came into existence because the Israelites sought a place to gather and celebrate their faith. The Tabernacle was a reminder that Israel was a congregation and not just separate families in individual tents.

Our passage comes immediately after a long list of rules for priests, laws about uncleanness, and instructions for those taking the Nazirite vow. (Samson is probably the best-known Old Testament figure who took the Nazirite vow. See Judges 13:5.) Immediately following this passage is a long account of who brought what gifts to the Tabernacle. This list is as exciting as a list of donors to a modern-day college or hospital.

However, right in the middle of this tedious passage comes a marvelous and gracious gift from God to God's people: the blessing. We use this passage most often as a benediction. These words have been set to music, spoken from pulpits, and memorized by children. This blessing promises that not only will God protect and keep the children of Israel, God will show them favor. The phrases "make his face to shine upon you" and "lift up his countenance upon you" both indicate that these people have found favor with God.

In addition, the priests are instructed to put God's name upon the people of Israel. The people of the Old Testament placed a great deal of importance on their names. They believed that the meaning of one's name would come to pass. To be called the people of God, to carry God's name, promised fulfillment of all God's gracious promises. Once a blessing was spoken, it could not be retracted.

These words of blessing were to come to the people of Israel, not through Moses, the leader God had chosen to take them from Egypt, but through the priests, those God had chosen to be in charge of the spiritual life of the Israelites. Spoken by the priests, the words of blessing would receive the power God had intended them to have.

The final promise in the blessing is that God will bring peace to the people called by God's name.

WORDS FOR OUR TIME

More and more our society is beginning to understand that it is impossible to live with only part of our life in good health. We have come to new understandings about the part our emotions and our minds play in regard to our physical bodies. We realize that only when our spiritual life is in balance with the rest of our life are we whole beings. This understanding began to develop as early as Moses' time. The Hebrew understanding of peace or *shalom* is to live one's entire life in harmony with God and with other people. When someone greets you by saying "Shalom," that person is asking for blessing on you.

In a larger sense the people of God live in the hope and promise of complete peace. Few signs point to the possibility that we as a global society will ever be able to achieve a time of peace. As Christians we need to order our lives so that we encourage a peace-filled reply to events that usually precipitate an angry response. In teaching our children that words are better than fists and that compromise is acceptable—even desirable—we lay the groundwork for these children to become national and international leaders who can bring about peace.

Perhaps the greatest barrier to personal peace and world peace is our failure to understand that peace comes through God. We consider ourselves basically self-sufficient. We believe that, if nothing else, our scientific technology will take care of us. But it cannot. We need God's blessing. When we truly accept that fact, we will have a different perspective on our relationship with our friends, coworkers, families, churches, communities, and world.

WORDS FOR MY LIFE

The blessing in the Book of Numbers comes only after the listing of several laws. God has always sought an obedient and righteous people. At times we would like to believe that the only thing expected is for us to love God. What we need to remember is that when we truly love someone, we respond to that person in a faithful manner. If we truly love our spouses, we honor them by our actions and remain faithful to them. If we truly love our children, we will set limits and help the children grow within those limits. If we love our friends, we will remain loyal no matter how their circumstances change. And if we love our God, we will be faithful to God and live in response to God's love. In other words, we do not give our time, talents, and gifts to the church to encourage God to love us. We already have God's love. We do not even do those things so God will see how good we are or so that others will see how good we are. God already knows just how good—and bad—we are. God loves us anyway. We need not be concerned about what others think as long as we are faithful to God. Anything we do that is an act of right living is a way of praising and blessing God. We give of our time, money, and talents in our churches or our communities because we realize that we need and want to give back in some small measure part of that with which God has blessed us.

We all have areas in our lives where we may feel that we do not have God's blessing. One of the great comforts of being children of God is that we can always ask God for what we need. If there is an area in your life that you feel needs to be touched by God's gracious blessing, go to God and ask for that blessing. Just as your pastor may ask for God's blessing on the words that he or she preaches, each of us should be comfortable asking for God's blessing on our chosen vocation, on our personal relationships, and on our times of "re-creating" ourselves. In our passage from the Book of Numbers, nothing says that God was required to give the blessing to the Israelites. The blessing is given freely by a God who is filled with concern and compassion for the people who have followed God into the desert. When a blessing is given so freely, we can receive it just as freely and celebrate it as a unique and wonderful gift.

7

The Unconditional Covenant
2 Samuel 7

I will be his father, and he shall be my son. When he commits iniquity, I will chasten him with the rod of men, with the stripes of the sons of men; but I will not take my steadfast love from him, as I took it from Saul, whom I put away from before you. And your house and your kingdom shall be made sure for ever before me; your throne shall be established for ever.

2 Samuel 7:14-16

WORDS FOR BIBLE TIMES

David had a special relationship with God. No other passage in the entire Old Testament speaks to the uniqueness of that relationship as does this one. Here is a covenant—but a unique covenant. All other covenantal relationships in the Old Testament include expectations for both parties. God promises certain things *if* the Israelites do as God commands. Yet the words of this passage, brought to King David through the prophet Nathan, contain no "if." God establishes the relationship of father and son. God then promises that while David and his descendants will be disciplined if they sin, never will they lose God's steadfast love. Even more, on a much more humanly understood level, God promises to David and his descendants that their "throne" will be made sure forever. The promise is not for one or two generations. This promise is good forever.

Second Samuel 7 opens with David's kingdom at peace. David realized that he had a house to live in; but the ark of God, believed to be God's dwelling place, remained in a tent. David proposed to the prophet Nathan that he now be allowed to build a proper house for God. At first Nathan agreed. But during the night the word of God came to Nathan, saying in effect, "If I wanted a house, I'd ask for one. Tell David I've been moving about with my people this whole time, and I'll decide when I settle down. It will be David's son who builds a house for me."

David's monarchy was the beginning of the golden age of the people of Israel, and he is held up as a model ruler. Kings until the time of the Exile would be measured in relation to David. (See, for instance, 2 Kings 14:3.) He was called "a man after [God's] own heart" (1 Samuel 13:14). David was by no means either a perfect man or a perfect king. He was a liar and an adulterer, and he orchestrated the murder of his lover's husband. Yet in the life of this imperfect man, God established a promise, an unconditional covenant, like nothing ever given before. God's love for God's people is based on much more than we as humans ever see in one another.

WORDS FOR OUR TIME

Like David, we seem to want a proper place for God's presence to dwell. When we were children, we entered church with a sense of quietness that was not present at our dinner tables or in our living rooms. As adults we continue to have a special feeling when we are inside our church. And yet God reassured David, and us, that God's presence does not need a special place in which to dwell. God's presence moved then and moves now in and among God's people.

After hearing the words of promise, David came to God

with a prayer that began with the words, "Who am I, O Lord GOD, and what is my house, that thou hast brought me thus far?" (2 Samuel 7:18). We can learn a great deal from the way David approached God. At times we all feel put upon, or we are full of complaints about what is not happening in our lives or about what we do not have. Like David, we need to stop and be amazed at what we have, where we live, the freedoms we enjoy, and all the wonderful possibilities for our lives. Our nation has experienced many years of "rest from our enemies." We need to utter a prayer of thanksgiving for the land and times in which we live. Then we need to move in responsible ways to change unjust, oppressive conditions for people who live in situations that are not as good as ours.

In Hebrew the word for steadfast love is *hesed*. The closest we can come to understanding *hesed* is to know that it is like the love a parent has for a child. *Hesed* is the kind of love that cannot help loving. *Hesed* sustains and is faithful even when there is anger and/or pain involved. God's love is like that of a parent who will live the rest of his or her life unable and unwilling to stop thinking of and caring for his or her child, no matter how old the child becomes. That same parent will continue to adjust to meet the needs of the changing child.

WORDS FOR MY LIFE

What can you count on "forever"? When you begin to list those things that are the most dependable in your life, you will soon find that every one of them can be taken away and/or destroyed by the power of humankind—with the exception of the love and presence of God. No one and nothing can destroy God's love for us. God's love goes on forever, no matter what happens. Even if civilization as we know it were to be destroyed, God's love would survive.

Most of us have experienced or will experience times when we feel as though we are losing everything. These times may come when a relationship becomes destructive for us or for someone we love. These times may come when we lose a job or when a parent, child, or dear friend dies. We may have such a feeling when we are enduring a debilitating illness. Through all those times what is most important is that we hold on to the "forever" in our lives. That "forever" is God's love, given to us in the extraordinary gift of Jesus Christ.

Do you ever stand amazed, as David did, by the unconditional love God has for you? Do you ever wonder why God has chosen you to be so blessed, so cared for? What is your response to such unconditional love? If we ever seek a relationship with God like David had, we must remember that David, in spite of all his sins, always knew when to say, "I'm sorry. I've sinned. Please forgive me." To be a person after God's own heart does not mean being morally perfect. We can see that by looking at David's imperfect life. Perhaps we need to remember that God is the One who decides where God will live and move, and we are the ones who must come to God when we need forgiveness. God's heart is open to those who come to God of their own free will and who then live in faithful response to God's goodness.

8

My Redeemer Lives
Job 19:25-27

For I know that my Redeemer lives,
and at last he will stand upon the earth.

Job 19:25

WORDS FOR BIBLE TIMES

The story of Job brings out in the open one of the theological questions asked most often: Why do innocent people suffer? Similar stories, using other characters and other gods, are also found in ancient Sumerian, Egyptian, and Babylonian writings. Job's questions are universal questions about suffering and pain and the place that God has in all that.

The background to this passage begins with a description of Job as a righteous, prosperous, God-fearing person. When God called the sons of God together, Satan was part of the group. God took a few minutes to brag on Job, pointing out how blameless and upright Job was. Satan's response was, in effect, "Well, of course he's God fearing! You've put a hedge around him, protected him from everything evil, and made his life pretty cushy!" God then gave Satan the power to do anything he wanted to Job—except kill him.

Then follows an account of Job's rapid decline. He lost his children, his wealth, his health, and his reputation. His friends all presented him with preposterous suggestions, each of them saying that Job must have done something to deserve such punishment; and if not, then surely he should curse God for this awful situation. Job listened each time; but he always came back with a response that God was somehow in the midst of this; and no, he did not think he had done anything that God had cause to punish.

Job 19:25-27 comes immediately after Job's third "friend" visits him. Job has just asked his friend Bildad why he at least cannot have pity on Job. Then come the words of angry hope and affirmation: "For I know that my Redeemer lives" (Job 19:25).

The people of Israel believed that if they did good, God would bless them; and if they did evil, God would punish them. This understanding of God was the basis for such evaluations of situations as, "Well, he's doing pretty well for himself. He's blessed; therefore, he must be good." Or the reverse, "I've never seen such terrible suffering. It must be that he is being punished for some evil he's done." So it was that Job's three friends tried to convince Job that he was being punished for evil or unrighteous deeds. If not, then God was not just; and Job should curse God and die. Throughout his pain and anger Job was unable to accept the view that he was being punished for committing evil deeds. He questioned God again and again but could not accept his condition as "punishment" for something he had done.

WORDS FOR OUR TIME

We all find it easy to ask "Job kinds" of questions. Many of us unfold the newspaper each day wondering what kind of atrocities have happened in our world during the night. In the midst of massacres, famines, plane crashes, and natural disasters, it is normal for us to cry out, "Where is God in all this?" We ask such questions because we want to believe that God is active and moving in history—in the history we are making today. But when we believe that God is active in history, we must face the question, "Is God then part of the evil that befalls us or others? Does it mean that God loves us less if we suffer?" Those questions can be considered at a national as well as at a personal level. Because we are living in peace, does that mean God accepts the way we dispense either justice or injustice?

We have often perceived justice as retribution; that is, those who deserve to be punished get punished. On the other hand, we also want to believe that our lives, blessed and cared for, are justly and deservedly good. Both those senses of justice are affronted when someone whom we think deserves to be punished is not and when someone who is innocent suffers. Why was Adolf Hitler allowed to live and destroy millions of people? Why must a six-year-old child die of AIDS acquired from a blood transfusion?

Somewhere in the midst of these struggles we have to reach the point of faith that Job had—that over and through all this God still is the loving, caring God we want and need. God has never promised that we will not suffer. During the time of the Exodus, God actually hardened Pharaoh's heart, making the suffering of the Hebrew people greater for a while. And in the unconditional covenant with David, God promised that when David sinned, he would be punished "with the rod of men, with the stripes of the sons of men" (2 Samuel 7:14). But that did not mean then and does not mean now that God abandons us in our times of suffering.

We also need to realize that when we are not suffering, we should not sit by complacently. Job's friends were not helpful and supportive of Job at all. All they did was find fault with him and make suggestions about what he must have done wrong. When people suffer, we need to find ways to make a difference. We may have the opportunity to send clothing to a disaster area. We may need to write to our representatives in Congress to impose sanctions against countries whose governments are oppressive.

WORDS FOR MY LIFE

Suffering brings a response. Secondary suffering also brings a response. Secondary sufferers are those who walk the journey of suffering with others. They are parents, spouses, children, and dear friends of those who are suffering directly. All of us at some time in our lives have been or will be exposed to someone who has suffered pain or illness or a loss of relationship. What should our response be to those who suffer? Sometimes merely our presence and our concern are enough. A little girl once came back from vacation and learned that her friend's cat had died. The child was quite upset that she had not been there when the animal died. The little girl's mother said, "But honey, there's nothing you could have done." The little girl responded, "I could have cried with her." Often when grief is shared, it becomes more tolerable.

Our response as secondary sufferers is to be there and to be the persons to whom those who are suffering can express their anger, fear, and pain. We should not be like Job's friends who tried to judge him. Our judgments will seldom be helpful and are probably not wanted or needed. The secondary sufferer needs to be a person who can strengthen the sufferer and help him or her deal with the suffering.

Some people who are suffering seem to draw more strength from God than they ever have. When we are not the ones suffering, we find it hard to understand how the pain (emotional and/or physical) can draw these people closer to God. These persons do not need us to understand their response, however. They need our celebration and support of their response. People who are dealing with serious illness, death, and emotional pain may make statements regarding God's presence in their situation that astonish us. It is a dear friend who realizes which of those statements need to be affirmed and which need to be challenged.

We do not get to the end of the story of Job in this passage. But at the end of the account Job comes to the understanding that he is asking the wrong question. Job had no right to ask, "What have I done? Why is this happening to me?" Instead, we all need to get to the point of asking, "How can I stay in right relationship with God through this?" For in the end that is all we have to hold on to: the loving, faithful relationship of God to God's people.

9

My Help Comes
From the Lord
Psalm 121

M y help comes from the LORD,
who made heaven and earth.
Psalm 121:2

WORDS FOR BIBLE TIMES

Psalm 121 is a psalm for travelers. It may have been
used on the way to or coming home from one of the
great feasts in Jerusalem. This psalm's comfort and assurance are not only spiritual, however; it promises protection. God's people will reach their destinations safely
because the creator God will protect them.

> I will lift up my eyes to the hills.
> From whence does my help
> come?

The question seems simple, maybe even rhetorical. However, we need to remember that after the reigns of David
and Solomon a split occurred in the nation. Ten tribes
became Israel, the Northern Kingdom; and two tribes
became Judah, the Southern Kingdom. Jerusalem, where
the Temple was located, was in the southern part of the
divided land. Those from the north had to make a long
and dangerous journey in order to go there to worship
God. So King Jeroboam in the north established "high
places," other shrines; and he invited God's people to

worship there. Many of these shrines became places where the Hebrew people worshiped false gods. So the question was a real question. Which god does help really come from? The answer of the psalmist is "the LORD," the God of the Hebrews, not a Baal of the Canaanites.

Psalm 121 contains a one-verse question, then seven verses of assurance. The words may have been chanted by faithful pilgrims as they left Jerusalem and made their way toward home. Such a journey produced great fears. The travelers faced not only the possibility of attack by robbers and villains but also the effects of the hot sun in the desert. Travel at night brought its own risks. Many people believed that the power of the moon could cause leprosy or lunacy. As the pilgrims walked through the hills and rough country, their fears could be put to rest by remembering that God was in control of the creation God had made.

The psalms were well-known by the time of Jesus' birth. Imagine the young couple, the wife very pregnant, as they journeyed to Bethlehem to be counted in the census. Did the words of this psalm echo through their minds as they traveled along the road that wound through the mountains? Did Joseph and Mary say the words aloud to each other when they were afraid? Twelve years later did the child Jesus join in reciting this psalm as he made his trip to Jerusalem with the rest of the faithful Jews to observe Passover? And did Mary and Joseph again speak these words as they returned, with hearts pounding, to Jerusalem to look for the boy who had been left behind?

WORDS FOR OUR TIME

Each of us can probably recall a time when we were first overwhelmed with the thought, *I am just a tiny bit of God's creation.* God's majesty in creating this world is almost more than we can comprehend. Often a child's very early perception is of being part of this wonderful world and yet how insignificant! But another thought shapes the human spirit. Surely the God who created the mountains will not cause our foot to stumble. And surely that God will never sleep and leave us unprotected.

Some of us have mountains to gaze out on. Others of us see prairies or cities. In our times it may be difficult to lift up our eyes to perceive God as keeper. Of course we understand that the moon does not cause leprosy or lunacy or AIDS. But we fear those things we do not understand, those things doctors and engineers do not understand. We still need reassurance that we are kept by God, that God can—and chooses to—protect and keep us. We can trust the God who has protected God's people again and again since the time of the Israelites.

And yet it is so hard to measure God's love by the customary ways we add up our security. There is no interest to record in a passbook, no promotion to a better job—only our belief that God cares about us and for us. We need to go, poetically if not literally, to where we are confronted with the power and majesty of creation. Then we have some understanding of the power and greatness of the God we worship.

We tend to trust more in things we can see, such as a strong military defense system, than in the things we cannot see, such as God's love for us. Yet nothing is more tangible, more real, than God's love.

The Israelites based their faith in God on more than a possibility that God would care for them. They had made their trips to and from great celebrations in Jerusalem in safety for years. They had given birth and fought wars. They had planted crops and brought in the harvest. They had experienced God's protection, both individually and as a nation. They could recite the words of this psalm with true confidence and assurance that their trust was not misplaced.

WORDS FOR MY LIFE

Each time the Hebrews made their journeys to and from Jerusalem and recited this psalm together, they asked the question, "From whence does my help come?" And each time they needed to decide. So do we. Where does our help come from? We are not always willing to say, "from the LORD, who made heaven and earth." Many of us have felt separated from God's love, alienated by our pain or struggles. We may crave the assurance that God loves us and yet not find it. At times like those each of us needs a secret mountain in our spirit. As the Hebrews made their journeys to and from Jerusalem, they had time to think. While they may have spent time chatting with one another along the way, they also had ample time to walk alone, to consider their own lives and their own relationships, especially their relationship with God.

When we feel that we are far from God, we need to find our own "mountain," the place where we find our own personal awareness that God is real. What kind of location reminds you that God cares for you in a unique and special way? For some people the secret place will be a place in God's natural creation, an actual mountain or a valley. Others will feel God's presence through music or a painting. Some of God's people will experience God's presence and a sense of assurance through the exerted energy of a distance run, the birth of a child, or a moment of aloneness.

The Israelites as a community also experienced God. As a group they had common understandings and goals. The Hebrews made their journeys to Jerusalem together, understanding that together they stood a better chance of making it safely to their destination than they did alone. That is a powerful lesson we must not forget. The person who says, "I don't need to go to church to worship God" is only a tiny bit right. The power of the litanies, prayers, and music shared by God's people can bring many of us to find our mountain. We express our identity and affirm one another's identity as people of God. We too stand a better chance of making it safely to our destination if we support one another instead of walking alone.

10

Whither Shall I Go From Thy Spirit?
Psalm 139

O LORD, thou has searched me and known me!
Thou knowest when I sit down and when I
  rise up;
thou discernest my thoughts from afar.

Psalm 139:1-2

WORDS FOR BIBLE TIMES

Psalm 139 expresses the fact that God knows all and is always present. This understanding seems quite normal to us, but early Judaism did not view God as all-knowing and ever-present. That conviction came later in its history. Yet in this psalm the writer has put in concrete language a special understanding of God's greatness and power.

This psalm is about the relationship that exists between Creator and creature. This psalm clearly announces that God is everywhere. No matter where God's creatures may go, they will not be away from God. In verse 8 the writer even announces that God will be in Sheol, the place of the dead. This teaching was a mature insight for the Israelites. Other passages, even in the Book of Psalms, say that God is not in the "pit" or Sheol. For example, Psalm 16:10 seems to portray God as outside the confines of "the pit" or Sheol.

Along with recognizing God's all-seeing and inescapable presence, this psalm contains a beautiful three-verse passage (verses 13-15) on God's creative activity forming us before we were born. From the making of our fingernails on, God has known every inch of our bodies.

This psalm takes a different direction in verses 19-22. Many times the writers of the psalms, as well as the writers of other passages, ask for God's help in defeating their enemies. Here the psalmist is almost ready to go to battle for God against those who refuse to worship a God so wonderful and majestic. The writer has no doubt that God will find this "perfect hatred" (Psalm 139:22) acceptable.

In the end the writer speaks humbly to God about imperfections that may be hidden somewhere deep inside him (Psalm 139:24). He asks that God help him recognize those sins and lead him "in the way everlasting" (Psalm 139:24).

This psalmist gives us a wonderful model of openness with God. He believes that no matter what he does or where he goes, not only will God's presence go with him, God will continue to protect him because God loves him. Even though the psalmist realizes he is imperfect, he does not question God's love for him. Rather, he seems to take comfort in having a relationship in which the Almighty knows him completely and in spite of any imperfections loves him absolutely.

WORDS FOR OUR TIME

A little saying goes, "I'm OK. God doesn't make junk." In a much more sophisticated and beautiful manner, this psalm asserts the same thing. If God had a hand in making us and knew from the beginning all that we are, then God loves us as we are.

One of the greatest gifts we can give our children and grandchildren is a healthy sense of self-esteem. If children believe in themselves, they can accomplish anything they set out to do. This psalm is a celebration of high self-esteem. We as adults need to stand back, look in the mirror, and say, "I am beautifully and wonderfully made!"

In this psalm the writer has taken time to reflect on God's presence, goodness, and creative power. We can learn great things from people who take time to sit and reflect and maybe put into words, if possible, their awareness of God in their lives. Our lifestyles now are so busy and so hectic that we do not take or make the time to consider how God is at work in and through us. We do not take time to consider what gifts God has given us. If we were to list all the gifts God has bestowed on us, we would be amazed. We would probably start thinking in general terms about having good health or a sharp mind and then move into detailed thoughts about our gifts.

We all have some creative powers, whether they be obvious like music or dance, or more hidden, like an affinity for working with older adults or with the very young. Perhaps we have the ability to go into chaotic situations and organize them, or perhaps for us balancing a checkbook is fun. All those abilities are gifts—precious, unique, and personal—given by God. They are not to be set aside in a corner but are to be used and polished and made the best they can be.

The only way we will realize our gift potential is to take time to discover it. Then we must celebrate it and use it. "Take time? When I'm so busy now with my job and the committees I sit on? What about my family and the yard work and the laundry and the clean house?" While we all have such responsibilities, we also have a responsibility to God to take the time to become more aware of God's presence and guidance in our lives.

WORDS FOR MY LIFE

If we accept the fact that God is the One who made us, then we must also accept the fact that God made others with their gifts as well. One of the strengths of the fellowship of Christians is the way we can encourage one another's gifts. Often we can see things in other people's lives that are gifts, but they do not necessarily recognize them as unique and special. When we affirm these people and help them build up their gifts, we are encouraging God's creative power in others.

Sometimes there are people in our lives whom we do not like, people with whom we are not comfortable. We especially need to recognize that God created those people and that they have special gifts and abilities. We need to realize that environmental situations or sometimes illnesses may change the way those gifts are or are not used. But the potential for using those gifts to God's glory is in each and every person. We are not the ones to judge if a person is acceptable to God. God is the One whose "eyes beheld my unformed substance" (Psalm 139:16). If God can love each person, then we can too.

We can take a large measure of comfort in this psalm that asserts,

> Whither shall I go from thy Spirit?
>   Or whither shall I flee from thy
>   presence?
> If I ascend to heaven, thou art there!
>   If I make my bed in Sheol, thou art
>   there!
>   (Psalm 139:7-8)

If we are in the doctor's office expecting bad news, God is there. If we are rejoicing with a friend over a promotion or a birth, God is there. Not even our worst thoughts are hidden from God. And God loves us, no matter what we think.

None of these understandings negates the fact that persons who work wickedness are part of life. Our responsibility is not to judge them but to stand firm for our beliefs, even when doing so threatens to cost us dearly in terms of relationships, business, and even family.

Our task needs to be like that of the psalmist when he asks for God's examination and guidance. As we examine our motives about why we do or do not take on a particular responsibility, we need to say to God, "Search me, God, and know my heart. Try me, and know my thoughts." If we do that, we will always respond from love and respect rather than from greed or lust for power.

11

A Voice in the Wilderness
Isaiah 40:1-11

In the wilderness prepare the way of
the LORD,
make straight in the desert a high-
way for our God.
Every valley shall be lifted up,
and every mountain and hill be
made low;
the uneven ground shall become level,
and the rough places a plain.
And the glory of the LORD shall be
revealed,
and all flesh shall see it together,
for the mouth of the LORD has
spoken.

Isaiah 40:3-5

WORDS FOR BIBLE TIMES

Most scholars believe the Book of Isaiah has two major parts. Isaiah 1–39 contains passages written in Judah by Isaiah himself. Chapter 40, the scholars tell us, begins the work of an unknown prophet, written about two centuries later. This so-called "Second Isaiah" lived in Babylon during the Exile.

Isaiah 40 is one of the most hope-filled chapters of the

Bible. The people of Judah have been in captivity in
Babylon. But a new voice now promises a new beginning,
a glorious journey back to Jerusalem, back into covenant
with God. The original Isaiah (Chapters 1–39) had
denounced the unrighteous acts of the people of Judah and
predicted that God's judgment would fall upon them.
"Second Isaiah" emphasizes the faithfulness of God and
God's loving response toward people who have suffered
enough.

The people of Judah must have doubted the prophet's
words. These people had learned to live in exile. Jerusalem, the burned-out city with the Temple in ruins, was a
painful memory for the oldest among them. Younger
adults, born in captivity, probably had no expectations
that they would ever again be a people with their own
city, their own place of worship, and their own land.

Memories had become entangled with legends, both
bringing a great deal of pain. The Temple and the Holy
City, Jerusalem, had been destroyed. Most of the people of
the city had been taken off in chains, led to Babylon in
humiliation. Only "the poorest of the land," who were too
sick, too old, or too crippled to be productive, were left in
the burned-out city (2 Kings 25:11-12).

Once they were in Babylon, the people of God had no
place to worship, no place to gather as a group of people
with an identity. They were prisoners of war who had
adapted in various ways so they could survive in a foreign
culture. "Why," many must have asked, "should we put
our hope in a defeated God?"

Then the word came that Judah would be led back to
Jerusalem in triumph. Everyone should watch the people of
Judah. If so, they would see the glory of the Lord who had
come to save this people. In Isaiah 40:10 God is portrayed
as a mighty commander of an army that will rescue God's
people. In verse 11 the imagery switches to that of a
shepherd—feeding his flock, carrying the lambs in his
arms, and leading the young in the right way. This God
would be strong and militant, rescuing his people when
that was necessary. This God would be a caring leader,
picking up the young and taking Judah's people safely
home.

WORDS FOR OUR TIME

These words of comfort would have meant little had they come before the Exile. Until people have experienced pain, they have little need for comfort. Many kinds of exile and many levels of pain exist. Corporate pain is the suffering of an entire group of people. In Babylon the people of Judah experienced corporate pain, as would the Jews of Germany centuries later. They suffered as individuals; but they also suffered as a people.

Whenever a war occurs, an entire nation of people is affected. The United States was so stunned by the Vietnamese War that more than a decade went by before the public was able to deal with the reality of what happened. Finally, a few "voices in the wilderness" began finding ways to comfort those who fought there and those who lost loved ones.

Isaiah 40:1-11 shows that the way of deliverance is God's alone. Only God can work salvation, and only God can decide when it is time to set people free from oppression. But others can "prepare the way" for that to happen. In what ways can we prepare the way for suffering people to be comforted? During times of illness and grief, only God can bring true comfort to those who are in pain. Yet we can prepare the way by reaching out and meeting the basic, everyday needs of persons who are suffering. For example, we can establish and be part of caring groups. We can provide rides, meals, child care, and laundry service for those who are going through hard times. Such simple acts prepare ways for God's Spirit to minister to persons in pain.

The unnamed prophet in Babylon promised his people almost a second Exodus. Again God's people had lived in a state of slavery, and again in God's own good time God would deliver them. No one is more grateful than someone who has been saved from disaster, not just once, but twice. When we look at the history of our country, we see that we have been spared and blessed so often that we should rejoice doubly, if not more. And yet there is so much left to do. Even though we have more college graduates than ever before, we also have a massive number of people in our country who do not read well enough to answer an ad for a job. How can God bring about deliverance from the oppression of illiteracy? Is it my responsibility to help? Each of us must answer those questions.

WORDS FOR MY LIFE

The people of Judah experienced exile in a physical, emotional, and spiritual sense. Physically, they were taken away from their homes, the Temple, and often from their families. Spiritually, they believed God had also been taken from them. Most of the people still did not understand that God was everywhere. When God's house (the Temple) was destroyed and the ark captured, the logical conclusion was that God was destroyed or captured too. In their tradition Jerusalem had been considered the only proper place to worship.

We may not be in physical exile, but we and others around us experience exiles of our own. We may not be banished from our country, but often we feel separated from the people who care about us. Any kind of broken relationship between spouses, between parents and children, or between longtime friends becomes a kind of exile. Persons dying from AIDS probably feel as though they are in exile, especially when they lose their jobs and are shunned by a frightened society, isolated from everyone and everything that could give them comfort.

To any of us who experience pain, this passage of Scripture offers hope and joy. Someone is out there who commands an invisible army ready to come to our rescue. Someone is out there who is the shepherd, ready to lift us gently, to nurture us, to care for our every need.

What experiences in your life have caused you to feel exiled? Maybe the loss of a job brought a strange new land of interviews and waits for telephone calls. Maybe you have known a loved one who left home angrily and seems as distant as if he or she were in a different country. Whatever your exile, hear in these words of Scripture the assurance that God delivers and brings God's people home in peace.

12

Wings Like Eagles
Isaiah 40:12-31

They who wait for the LORD shall
    renew their strength,
they shall mount up with wings like
    eagles,
they shall run and not be weary,
    they shall walk and not faint.

Isaiah 40:31

WORDS FOR BIBLE TIMES

Exile brought an emptiness, almost a barrenness, that left the people feeling powerless and far from God. Not only did the Jews in Babylon feel powerless, many of them were seriously tempted to give up their ethnic identity and worship the Babylonian gods.

The civilization the people of Judah experienced in Babylon was like nothing they had ever seen. The buildings were magnificent, especially the temples. And there were statues of the Babylonian gods. The Hebrews could easily see how these gods looked, unlike their God whom they had never seen. Foods were prepared with no attention to Hebrew dietary laws, yet the foods were delicious. To become Babylonians would be so easy. And some Jews did. By no means did all the Hebrews choose to return to Jerusalem when many years later they had the chance to do so.

The words of Isaiah 40:12-31 present us with several

metaphors. Hope can be articulated by metaphors but must be based in concrete experience. The prophet spoke in metaphors about God as a person in business who carefully and honestly measured the waters in the hollow of his hand, marked off the heavens with a span, and weighed the mountains in scales and the hills in a balance (Isaiah 40:12). The metaphor in verses 22-23 portrays God as a builder whose production stretches across the skies, dwarfing humans to where they look like grasshoppers. In verses 28-29 this Creator is presented as everlasting, inexhaustibly strong, with wisdom beyond human comprehension. If the members of the exiled community think their God has forgotten them, verse 26 invites them to look skyward. All those stars! God knows and guides each one of them. God has not forgotten God's people in their captivity.

WORDS FOR OUR TIME

While hope can be articulated in metaphorical language, the experience of hope must be based in concrete reality. The people of Judah could believe that God was everything that the prophet promised because they were a people with a memory of hope. They remembered the story of Joseph. He could face his brothers and say, "You meant evil against me; but God meant it for good" (Genesis 50:20). They remembered the promise given to David, those incredible words *for ever* (2 Samuel 7:16).

The people of Judah had been invited to hope; so have we. To hope is to believe that things can be different and that the difference will be better.

We can realize that exile for us may be any situation of despair—caused by relationships or finances or corrupt authorities. Sometimes our hopelessness prevents our seeing any way things could be better. At such times we need new eyes and a new imagination. In the middle of the Exile, Isaiah 40 showed that God was calling on the people of Judah to envision a new possibility.

That new imagination could bring laughter where before there was only emptiness. It could bring joy where sadness was the only response before. That new imagination brings life back to the place where there had been death, like hearing the news that one is in total remission from cancer or realizing that one has complete movement again after a stroke. Hope is the food basket brought to a housing project the night before Thanksgiving—when the only nourishment the people had expected for the next day was macaroni and cheese.

Our world gives us much about which to feel despair. The prophet of Isaiah 40 helps us understand that we are not children of this world, we are children of God. We are not children of inside traders and drug dealers. We are not children of those who smuggle armaments or hide truths. We are the sons and daughters of the God who provides a strong arm to the powerless while bringing the powerful to their knees.

WORDS FOR MY LIFE

We must be careful in speaking words of hope to friends and family who are in pain, however. We should not move from pain to hope too quickly. Remember that between Isaiah 39 and Isaiah 40 were nearly two hundred years of experience. There was time for the people of Judah to accept their pain and to try to deal with it. They had time to acknowledge how hurt and afraid they were and how they doubted God's presence and power. Pain had washed over them like the grief of a parent at a child's funeral. Out of seemingly endless grief comes the opportunity for words of hope to convey new joy.

We need to understand that the prophet who spoke these words did not approach a despair-filled people from the outside to bring them words of hope. Rather, the prophet too had shared the experience of pain and grief. Only those who really have experienced pain can come close to understanding another's pain and the needs that arise from it. While we may be hypocritical if we say "I know just how you feel" to someone who is in his or her own particular grief, we can remember whatever pain we have known and through that memory reach a compassion that helps heal.

Hope, as well as creating a new imagination, provides power and freedom. Power comes as God shows us how to take control of our situations. The exiles in Babylon seemed to have no control of their own lives. But the promise of the prophet was that they would soon be out from under the thumb of the Babylonian royalty. They could remember their relationship of child to parent with their God. A painful situation in which we have no control, such as the loss of a loved one, job, or health, makes us feel like prisoners. When we are able to take some measure of control over that situation, we are empowered. Perhaps there is no more beautiful metaphor for empowerment and freedom than that found in Isaiah 40:31. We need to wait. We cannot push God. In that waiting we need to recognize where God is. Then we will have the freedom of renewed strength. We will fly like eagles. We will run and never get that stitch in our sides. We will be able to walk up and down mountains if we choose and not be weakened. We will be filled with the power of God!

13

What Does the Lord Require?
Micah 6:6-8

He has showed you, O man, what is
good;
and what does the LORD require of
you
but to do justice, and to love kindness,
and to walk humbly with your God?

Micah 6:8

WORDS FOR BIBLE TIMES

To understand the power of these words, we need to know something about the Book of Micah as a whole. Micah lived in the eighth century B.C. He was from a village named Moresheth, located south of Jerusalem. In the first chapter of the book, we find a reference to the destruction of the Northern Kingdom (Micah 1:6-7), which occurred in 721 B.C. The fall of the north should have served as a warning for the people of the south. But just the opposite was true. Those in the south, particularly in Jerusalem, believed that they would always be safe because God had said, "I will put my name [in Jerusalem] . . . for ever" (2 Kings 21:4, 7). God's name was God's essential being. A city bearing God's name would seem to have a guarantee of protection.

Resting in that belief, the people of Judah began to corrupt the covenant by unrighteous and sinful living. In response, the writer of the Book of Micah boldly unmasked their sins, particularly those of the rich and powerful. He did not leave any group of prestigious people untouched. The politicians, the big landowners, the military leaders, even the other prophets and priests, are all accused of being greedy, of breaking the covenant, and of violating God's will for creation.

The three primary phrases in Micah 6:8 are "do justice," "love kindness," and "walk humbly with your God." To "do justice" did not mean to perform the job of a judge. *Justice* is a noun that refers to the duty of everyone to learn what God requires of him or her. For public officials in Micah's day that meant they were to do their duty fairly, no matter what the status of the people with whom they were dealing. For priests it meant keeping the liturgy and the worship faithful, speaking hard words in love if that was necessary. For parents it meant defining limits for their children and being sure those limits were observed.

The word *kindness* is best understood as loyalty to all that is right and good. Kindness means being faithful in marriage, in friendships, and in obedience to God. People who are kind do not oppress the poor. To oppress the poor would be to break the covenant.

To "walk humbly with your God" means to be obedient to God, whatever the demands. God judges wrongdoing. Micah was reminding his people that God was their Creator. God was in charge. Their responsibility was to stay in right relationship with the Almighty.

WORDS FOR OUR TIME

One of the things that most offended the prophet Micah was hypocritical worship and superficial religious ceremonies. Micah did not say that sacrifice and the burning of incense had no place in the religion of Judah. Micah observed people who came to worship and participated in all the religious ceremonies of the day. Their liturgies spoke of loving God and neighbor with all their heart. Then those same people went out and tampered with the scales they used in the marketplace. Micah said that to God such behavior was blasphemous. Worship is to be a response from us to God's faithfulness, a response that includes living the kind of life God would have us lead.

All churches need money to function, but to write a check to help the church when that money has been made by cheating other people can only be called injustice. The Book of Micah makes clear God's special love for the poor. When money is made by taking advantage of people, God is saddened and angered.

Right worship is a joy-filled response to God because we are so grateful we can do nothing except praise God. In addition, when we worship properly, we become concerned about the plight of those who live deep in anxiety because of their financial or emotional needs. When we leave worship, we are to live as the people of God, doing justice wherever we can.

God's love for us is overwhelming, forgiving, and stead-fast. God's love endures forever. God loves us in good times and in bad. The metaphor of parent is often used in describing God's love because it is one that many of us identify with easily. But, like a parent's love, God's love is not so sentimental that it overlooks wrongdoing. In fact, one of the primary responsibilities of a parent is to set limits and to hold a child to those limits. A parent must discipline a child when he or she misbehaves.

God's love for us is personal and individual, but God plays no favorites. God's love is for everyone. If one of God's people, God's creation, is hurt by another, God feels the pain. Between two children of the same parent injustice will occur. Correction is needed. God's out-reaching love is to a world full of God's children. Justice, kindness, and walking in humility become complicated. God cares about all those treated unjustly or unkindly and about those who show no humility as they strut before their sisters and brothers.

God sent the prophets to tell the people what they were doing wrong. The function the prophets played was not always popular, but it was essential. Prophets are at work in our time too. Are there not women and men who have made you see clearly the way God desires you to live? We are less likely to recognize prophets today than people were in Old Testament times. But God keeps sending prophets to us. Pastors, members of Congress, used-car dealers, entertainers, college professors, art teachers, and secretaries all can be prophets. They can make God's way clear and act out the righteous living God expects.

WORDS FOR MY LIFE

Where do you need to do justice? Is it at your place of work? in your neighborhood? in your family? How can you, one person, change unjust situations? To know what to do in such cases is never easy. We need to look deep down inside ourselves and find places where our own greed and self-centeredness take over and impede our attempts at justice. Any hypocrisy weakens our efforts to work for justice.

Hypocrisy is often associated with the issue of worship. Here we must be quite personal. No one sitting next to you in the pew will know if you are there in true worship or if you are there to be sure someone sees you. Some people belong to a church because it is the socially acceptable thing to do. Others belong because they know they may need the church for weddings or funerals. Some persons go to church because it is good for their children. We all need to sit down and prayerfully examine our motives for worship as well as our motives for working within the church in the fellowship of other Christians. Why do you teach Sunday school or cook for those who are ill? Why do you provide transportation for older adults or wrap gifts for nursing home residents at Christmas? Go one step further and ask, "Are my motives pure when I write a check or when I give of my own time and efforts?"

God's prophets have long called for the end of injustice. For each of us the decision to join the battle against injustice has to be made at a different time and place. Perhaps yours needs to be the voice that speaks up against an injustice you see in your workplace or community. We are the people of God. Therefore, we are responsible for all of God's creation; and God wants justice for all people—for persons who are not members of our local church, denomination, or faith as well as for those who are. We are all God's creatures. Only when there is justice for everyone will anyone truly experience justice.

14

When Jesus Was Born
Matthew 1:18–2:12

She will bear a son, and you shall call his name Jesus, for he will save his people from their sins.

Matthew 1:21

WORDS FOR BIBLE TIMES

The story of Jesus' birth as told by Matthew plays a very important role in the church's understanding of our Savior's life and ministry. Matthew's Gospel is more than a happy report of the birth of a child. Matthew has a much higher purpose. He is reminding us of God's faithful covenant love: a love so vast that it must be revealed in human history. The birth narrative in Matthew captivates us because it causes us to remember that God loves the world so much that God sent us a Savior!

Turning to our passage, we therefore see it as more than a recounting of historical events. In a sense, Matthew is writing more as a theologian than as a historian. He wants to tell us what God has done. So the purpose of our passage is to help establish in our minds the uniqueness of Jesus. Not only was he born in a special way, he was a special person. To help us understand how special Jesus was to Matthew, let us notice in this Gospel five descriptive titles given to our Lord.

First, our Lord is the **Savior** (Matthew 1:21). Eight days after his birth, during the rite of circumcision, Jesus received his name (Luke 2:21). The meaning of his name is quite significant. *Jesus* is the Greek form of a Hebrew word that means Yahweh (God) is salvation. Jesus is our salvation!

Second, our Lord is **Emmanuel**, "God with us" (Matthew 1:23). Here Matthew quotes from Isaiah 7:14. Some people think this title strikes at the heart of Matthew's Gospel: The living God, known as Creator, Judge, and Redeemer, has entered human history. God has become like us so we can become like God's Son. Christians call this marvelous act the Incarnation.

Third, our Lord is the **king of the Jews** (Matthew 2:2). The scholars from the East (the wise men) first called Jesus a king. And they were Gentiles! They recognized Jesus' divine royalty, a royalty that filled them with admiration and awe. To have Gentiles respond so fully to God's Son certainly means that all people are meant to receive God's good news. Human distinctions relating to race or national origin mean nothing to God.

Fourth, our Lord is the **Christ** (Matthew 2:4). The word *Christ* means to be anointed as God's Chosen One. This title is an obvious reference to Jesus as the God-chosen deliverer who was to come. Note that it was Herod who referred to Jesus as the Christ. If only he had realized what he was saying!

Fifth, our Lord is a **ruler** (Matthew 2:6). When Matthew quotes Micah 5:2, the stress is on the caring nature of Jesus' authority. Micah continued his description of this ruler by saying,

> He shall stand and feed his flock. . . .
> And they shall dwell secure.
> (Micah 5:4)

Jesus is no forceful ruler, uncompromising and tough. He is the Shepherd who cares for the sheep (his people). This idea from Micah also establishes an association of Jesus' rule with David's line, an important qualification for the messiah in the minds of many Jews.

No wonder the birth of Jesus was a remarkable event. He is a remarkable person! When has anything like this ever happened? "She will bear a son, and you shall call his name Jesus, for he will save his people from their sins" (Matthew 1:21).

WORDS FOR OUR TIME

In his fascinating memoirs *In My Father's Court* (Farrar, Straus & Giroux, Inc., 1966), Isaac Singer recalls figures from his boyhood years in Poland. He mentions a rabbi who slept fully dressed six nights a week. The rabbi did not want to waste precious time getting dressed should the messiah come while he was asleep. The rabbi was more relaxed on the sabbath night. After all, as he said, not even the messiah would come on such a holy day as the sabbath.

A wonderful sense of devotion, as well as of humor, is present in this delightful story. Life was hard in Warsaw before World War I. For many people the only real hope of a better life lay with the coming of the messiah. People felt a sense of emptiness about the way things were. If only the messiah would come, then everyone would be happy and dance in the streets. Then the rabbi could finally wear a nightshirt!

How often have we had similar feelings? Life is so full of stress: rush-hour traffic on the freeway, fast foods, and nights filled with television sitcoms. If only the messiah would come. Taxes are going through the roof. The world economy is a mess, and nobody can live in peace. If only the messiah would come. There is danger in the streets and temptation in the city. If only the messiah would come. Someone has to help us stabilize our lives. If only . . . .

It is a bit strange, isn't it, that we have many of the same feelings that the citizens of old Poland and the Jews in ancient Palestine had. If history and psychology teach us anything, it is that human hopes and fears remain much the same from generation to generation. Whether we travel by buggy or by rocket makes little difference. Life in any age has unanswered questions. We instinctively look for help.

The great lesson we learn from the Gospel of Matthew is that the world has not been abandoned. We are not left in the human struggle alone. The Messiah has come! In Jesus we are assured of God's available presence, of God's saving love. Yes, we have great needs; but we have a great God. God remembers the covenant made with our spiritual ancestors. In fact, the covenant is stronger than ever because God has come to us in the form of the Son. The beautiful thing is that we no longer have to say, "If only the Messiah would come."

For Christians things are not the same as they always were. Troubles and difficulties still abound, but a new mood has been created. A deep sense of joy and salvation has come. We do not have to strain to make our relationships, careers, and possessions provide meaning for us. Meaning and happiness have come. Life is changed. The Messiah has arrived!

Has your life taken a new turn with Christ? How does your faith enable you to live with joy in today's world?

WORDS FOR MY LIFE

Matthew's staggering announcement is that God has entered human history. The God who was made known in Creation, during the crossing of the Red Sea, through numerous miraculous deeds, and eventually through the prophets has done something new, something totally unexpected. God has come to us in our time and calls us to a personal commitment to God. Our Scripture passage is much more than a beautiful story; it is a claim on our lives.

This fact means that the coming of God in Jesus Christ calls us to make a choice. Will we reject him like Herod, who was inwardly angered by the thought of the birth of Jesus? Or will we be like the wise men, who were filled with joy and wonder? Just asking those questions gives us the answer. How can we possibly be angered and put off by the coming of a loving ruler who saves? How can we turn away from the Anointed One, from him who is God with us?

The coming of Christ is above all a personal event. He has come for us, for each of us individually. The personal character of Christ's coming speaks of several wonderful aspects of God's relationship with us. It tells us that God has entered into our feelings. God knows our joys, fears, sorrows, and trials. And since God made a choice to come in Christ, God made a choice *for us!*

The coming of Christ leads us to be open to God's daily grace in our lives. Jesus did not come into the world only to leave us alone again later. No, he came to remain with us (Matthew 28:20) and eventually to receive us into the Kingdom. Therefore, we can open ourselves every day to his presence and power and be assured of his faithful love.

A saintly writer once compared the human soul to warm wax waiting for a seal. This analogy is quite helpful. We are indeed waiting for some kind of identity, some sign of who we really are. The incarnation of God in Jesus Christ is that great seal. As soon as it is impressed on the soft wax of our hearts, we are marked as children of God. We then have a new and lasting identity in God. No wonder the message of the coming of Jesus Christ is good news!

15

The Lord's Prayer
Matthew 6:1-15

Our Father who art in heaven,
Hallowed be thy name.

Matthew 6:9

WORDS FOR BIBLE TIMES

The Lord's Prayer in the Gospel of Matthew is part of the Sermon on the Mount (Matthew 5–7). The outstanding teachings of Jesus in the Sermon on the Mount turn our eyes toward the life that pleases God. In the middle of the sermon Jesus talks of sincerity in the service of God. It is here, in the midst of Jesus' teaching on avoiding pride, that we find the Lord's Prayer, the single most highly regarded teaching of Jesus on prayer.

The Lord's Prayer is primarily concerned with our private prayers. The surrounding verses make it clear that Jesus is not speaking about public worship. He wants our private prayers to be acceptable to God, not opportunities for vain display. So Jesus gives us a model for the kind of prayer that pleases God.

First, prayer begins with praise (Matthew 6:9-10). The phrase "Our Father who art in heaven" acknowledges our proper relationship with God. God is our loving parent who fills heaven and earth. As a parent who loves us, God invites us to the intimacy of private prayer. And because we love God, we want God's name to be spoken in reverence, God's righteous rule (kingdom) to be manifested, and God's good will to be done by everyone. These three desires are really three acts of praise. All these things we ask to be done "on earth." A natural result of such universal reverence for God would be peace among all people. How wonderful that would be!

Second, having given God our praise, now we may bring our petitions to God (Matthew 6:11-13). Just as there are three acts of praise, there are also three general petitions. These are (1) give us our daily bread, (2) grant us forgiveness of sin, and (3) do not put us to a test too hard for us. The request in verse 13 to be delivered from evil is an extension of praying that we not be put to a difficult test. These petitions have deep meaning, especially when we remember that Matthew's Gospel has the kingdom of God as its special focus. To pray for daily bread is at the same time a request to be nourished at the Messiah's heavenly banquet in the Kingdom. Likewise, if we expect to be forgiven and admitted into the Kingdom, we must forgive. And we pray to be spared undue suffering in preparation for the coming of the Kingdom.

Third, our prayers should end with an affirmation of God's good plan for our lives. Normally we simply say "Amen," which means "so be it." This final doxology, "For thine is the kingdom . . ." is contained in a footnote in many versions of the Bible because it is not present in the oldest manuscripts. However, its use in the church dates from very early times. Regardless of the particular words we use to end our prayers, we should end them expressing our confidence in God's willingness to hear us and to bless us.

WORDS FOR OUR TIME

One of the most important acts of public worship for Christians is the pastoral prayer. At this point in the worship service, the pastor tries to sense and express the congregation's desire to praise God. The pastor also presents the congregation's needs to God, needs that are often personal and difficult to express. The pastoral prayer should be an intimate time of adoration and petition for each member of the worshiping community.

In spite of its value in worship, the pastoral prayer is a dangerous time. Without careful attention to what is happening, such prayer can become routine and lifeless. In the Sermon on the Mount, Jesus warns against insincerity in prayer (Matthew 6:5-8). Pastors must not let their public prayers become a stylized set of cliches or a time to remind the members of the congregation of their responsibilities. Happy the people whose leader sincerely prays from the heart!

Jesus labels as "hypocrites" those who use public prayers as opportunities for self-display (Matthew 6:5). The word *hypocrite* means actor, one who is playing a role. A hypocrite in prayer could be a person who is showing off or one who merely goes through the motions. Jesus never condemns genuine public worship. But he does say that true righteousness is most in evidence when we pray to God in private. Then our prayers are really addressed solely to God, who is willing to bless.

Writing to Titus, the apostle Paul urged him to "show yourself in all respects a model of good deeds, and in your teaching show integrity, gravity, and sound speech" (Titus 2:7-8). Integrity and gravity are based on sincerity. As Christians, we must conduct ourselves righteously and sincerely in all our relationships. This way of life is especially necessary today because in our society people tend to be suspicious of one another's motives.

A newspaper reporter discovered that a local politician privately supported a measure that he publicly opposed. Such hypocrisy tends to make us skeptical of politicians. As a nation, we long for honest and forthright leaders and for honesty in all our business relationships. People at all levels of society need to be aware that Jesus' concern for right prayer invades every aspect of our lives, calling for honesty and sincerity in all we say and do.

WORDS FOR MY LIFE

Jesus says that "when you pray, go into your room and shut the door and pray to your Father" (Matthew 6:6). Jesus emphasizes that God is in this kind of secret place. When we meet God in secret, God will hear our prayers and grant a blessing for our lives. The intimacy of private prayer is absolutely crucial to the development of a genuine spiritual life.

Why is private prayer so important? First of all, it establishes and then strengthens the bond between ourselves and God. Jesus teaches that God is a good parent, patient and caring. When we become aware of this fact, we can experience joy in prayer, being confident of God's deep love for us.

Second, private prayer helps us grapple with the tensions of life. Life is larger than we are, demanding more strength than we have. Moreover, we can never be sure of the turns life will take. Therefore, we need God's active presence in our hearts and minds. When we pray as God would have us pray, we find assurance that God will help us meet life victoriously.

Third, private prayer always gives us an opportunity to express our confidence in God's will. Trusting God, we say "Amen" to wherever God leads and to whatever God wants. The Lord's Prayer is a model of confidence in God's loving ways. By surrendering to God's ways, we are saying that we know that God will take us down the right path.

Have you ever thought of the Lord's Prayer as a working model for your own prayer life? Do you begin your personal prayer with an attitude of praise and thankfulness? Are you able to pinpoint your specific needs, as the Lord's Prayer does? Does the idea of forgiving others as a precondition of being heard yourself challenge you to repair relationships with others and to seek a deeper, more meaningful relationship with God? When you say "Amen" at the end of your prayer, does that mean you truly accept God's will and recognize your dependence on God's almighty power?

The thought that we are invited into prayerful union with God is both comforting and awe-inspiring. However unworthy we feel, we find God open to us through prayer. And Jesus makes plain the kind of prayer God likes: We are to pray sincerely, humbly, and with a childlike attitude toward the goodness of God. So let us take time daily for quiet, reflective prayer. If we do, we will find God's will being done in every area of our lives.

16

Forgiveness of Sins
Mark 2:1-12

"That you may know that the Son of man has authority on earth to forgive sins"—he said to the paralytic—"I say to you, rise, take up your pallet and go home."

Mark 2:10-11

WORDS FOR BIBLE TIMES

One of the strange ironies of the Gospels is the amount of hostility Jesus faced during the early days of his ministry. The irony is compounded when we realize that this opposition often came from the religious leaders. According to the Gospel of Mark it was Jesus' compassion, of all things, that drove him headlong into conflict with many of the religious leaders. The acts and teachings of Jesus did not fit neatly into their preconceived ideas, and that caused these people a great deal of tension. Certainly this story of the forgiving and healing of a man with a handicapping condition highlights this problem.

Mark 2:1-12 describes one of the most unusual events in the New Testament. Jesus was home in Capernaum (Mark 2:1), which was now his headquarters. The house was packed with people wanting to see him. In fact, people were packed so tightly that no more could enter. But this situation did not deter four clever fellows who were bringing their friend to Jesus. They climbed up on the roof, opened a hole in the ceiling, and lowered their friend in front of Jesus. The people in the crowd were wide-eyed. Jesus was impressed.

When Jesus looked at the man, he could see something no one else could see. So Jesus said, "My son, your sins are forgiven" (Mark 2:5). First, matters of the heart; then matters of the body. But on hearing Jesus' words, the religious leaders bristled and thought, *Who is this blasphemer to think he can forgive sins? Only God can do that!* Jesus remarked, "Why do you question thus in your hearts? Which is easier, to say . . . 'Your sins are forgiven,' or to say, 'Rise, take up your pallet and walk'?" (Mark 2:9). Turning to the man, Jesus said, "Rise, take up your pallet and go home" (Mark 2:11).

Interestingly enough, the attitude of the religious leaders contained a kernel of truth. No ordinary man could forgive sins. And that is Mark's point: Jesus is no ordinary man! The physical healing is simply a demonstration that Jesus has a deeper authority, the authority to deal with matters of the heart.

This passage of Scripture is about a Redeemer the religious leaders misunderstood because their judgment was clouded. Their traditions had blinded them to the greatest truth imaginable: Almighty God had come in Jesus Christ to redeem humankind. The Son of man was there, but the religious leaders could not take it in. So confusion had set in early in Jesus' ministry. This confusion would eventually lead to rejection and judgment (see Mark 3:6).

WORDS FOR OUR TIME

The story of this man with a handicapping condition is a prime example of why the Nicene Creed says that Jesus is "God from God, Light from Light, true God from true God . . . of one being with the Father."[1] These phrases affirm that Jesus is unique and beyond our powers to describe. Yet we can love and serve him as our Savior.

The modern church wants to make the same point that the Gospel of Mark and the Nicene Creed make: Jesus is the One who makes things right. The spirit of Jesus alive in human hearts can overcome the distressing problems of personal and social life.

Jesus gave primacy to the individual, not to the social order. Society exists for people; people do not exist for society. Deep in our hearts we know that Jesus was right.

Many employees are frustrated because they feel like helpless pawns being moved from place to place by gigantic corporate forces. Strikes and picket lines are strong testimony to our desire to be treated as persons who deserve respect. Consumers often protest when they are treated as little more than numbers on a computer chip.

Jesus showed mercy to the individual. In his day, especially among the Romans, mercy was regarded as weakness. The Romans believed that only the strongest should survive. This feeling is still around today, especially in inner city gangs and paramilitary groups. Jesus came to heal people, not to hurt them. And to heal them, Jesus identified with their poverty and powerlessness. The masses came to Jesus because they recognized in him a person who cared deeply about their plight. In a way the man with the handicapping condition represents all people who are victimized and manipulated. To the poor and destitute Jesus brings forgiveness and healing.

The heavy resistance Jesus faced came from the religious leaders. They represent a "don't-rock-the-boat" corporate mentality. They are the ones who criticize Jesus and ignore the man with the handicapping condition. They are blinded by their traditions, unable to evaluate clearly, especially in regard to Jesus. In sharp contrast, the common people rejoice over the mighty works of God that Jesus performed.

The church at its best today continues to be the champion of the common people. Christians believe it is Jesus who makes things right. Other means such as government policies, economic programs, and revolutionary power are stopgap measures at best. Only Christ can change people from the inside out. And only changed people can change society for the best.

WORDS FOR MY LIFE

Jesus still comes to us today, offering us the opportunity to have a personal relationship with him. The only question is, "What will our attitude be toward his mercy?"

Will we be like the religious leaders, having our hearts filled with doubt and judgment? These people were not his followers, they were his critics. These religious leaders become a warning to us. No denomination or system of doctrine, however good, is a substitute for a personal relationship with God.

Is it possible that we will be like the crowd of people who pushed their way into Jesus' house? They had heard of him and were curious. They listened as he taught. They realized that there was something special about him and praised God for his healing miracle. They stood in awe.

Perhaps we have the faith of the man with the handicapping condition and his companions. They simply would not be denied an audience with Jesus. Certainly their method was creative! But the four companions believed something wonderful would happen if they could just get their friend to Jesus. Do we have this kind of faith?

Each of us studying this passage of Scripture has some inner reaction to Jesus. We may doubt him, fear him, praise him, believe him. We cannot remain neutral. The gospel calls us to choose. Our spiritual lives—how we relate to God and what we expect from God—are based on our understanding of Jesus' life and work. This passage of Scripture turns us inward, making us face ourselves and Jesus. With his help we can identify our individual problems and call on his compassion for a cure.

The eternal truth of this passage of Scripture is that Jesus has the divine authority to forgive sins. Healing the body was merely a confirmation of that authority. We know the healed man later became sick again and died—as we all must. The great miracle was that Jesus made him a new man from within. When Christ does this for us, it is the greatest miracle!

The healed man and his companions went away happy. They had reached Jesus, and he had rewarded their faith. Since the Resurrection, Jesus Christ is immediately available to all of us. We do not have to go to a certain place to meet him. The caring, healing Christ is as close as our desire to touch him.

---

[1] From "The Nicene Creed," in *The United Methodist Hymnal* (Copyright © 1989 The United Methodist Publishing House); No. 880.

17

The Last Supper
Mark 14:12-25

As they were eating, he took bread, and blessed, and broke it, and gave it to them, and said, "Take; this is my body." And he took a cup, and when he had given thanks he gave it to them, and they all drank of it. And he said to them, "This is my blood of the covenant, which is poured out for many."

Mark 14:22-24

WORDS FOR BIBLE TIMES

Jesus and the disciples were in Bethany. On Thursday morning he sent Peter and John into Jerusalem (Luke 22:7-8). They were to make preparations for Jesus and the disciples to celebrate Passover later that evening. A friend had made an upper room available to the group. Having secured the room, Peter and John returned to tell Jesus that everything was ready. Soon they all left for Jerusalem. A sense of foreboding engulfed Jesus.

The dinner was going well. As host, Jesus was leading the disciples through the elaborate rituals of the Passover meal. The disciples were familiar with the details. They had kept the feast since they were children. Then, quite unexpectedly, Jesus dropped a bombshell: "One of you will betray me" (Mark 14:18). The disciples were horrified. What did he mean by that? Each man searched his soul, that is, everyone except Judas.

During the place in the meal when the Jewish family joined in eating the Passover lamb, Jesus did something unusual. He took bread, said the blessing, broke it, and called it his body. Then he gave the bread to his disciples to eat. Next he took a cup of wine, gave God thanks, and said it was his blood. Each man in turn drank from the cup. Jesus said that what he had done represented a new covenant with God. The bread and cup would be new symbols of God's presence. The disciples were quiet, for this had become a strange night.

The Passover was the most sacred feast of the Jews. By observing it, they recalled how God had delivered their ancestors from slavery in Egypt. They also remembered God's covenant that was established on Mount Sinai. The disciples probably thought of God's power and love and of the ancient promise of a messiah who would save the people. In the midst of remembering the old covenant, Jesus announced a new covenant. The disciples would not have been greatly surprised. They knew that Jesus was changing the old order.

The symbols of bread and cup for body and blood were troubling to the disciples. These symbols suggested sacrifice. Jesus was connecting his coming death with the new covenant. The disciples were to acknowledge this new teaching by eating the bread and by drinking from the cup. In some mysterious way Jesus' death would be the food of the Kingdom. Just as God established the old covenant, God's Son established the new covenant. But this time the covenant would not be for Israel alone. No, now it would be for "many"—an endless number, whoever will!

WORDS FOR OUR TIME

A social scientist in discussing American culture has said that we as a people are basically grasping and self-centered. He said that our preference for technology over persons, for production over values, confirms this fact. He pointed out that this new way of living is a drastic change from the frontier days when people had to depend on one another in order to survive. What America needs, he suggested, is a redirection of our social goals. We need once again to be a service-oriented nation rather than a product-oriented nation. How to make this change at this point in our national life is the question. In this case, the diagnosis is easier than the cure.

The church has been saying much the same thing for quite a long time. Resistance to the church's message has been strong, sometimes coming from within its own ranks. And what is the message of the church? Its message is that a kinder, gentler society comes with serious allegiance to Jesus Christ and his values. Human beings do not have to create this society by their own efforts alone. Persons who are deeply committed to Christ have found a supporting power that enables them to live as Jesus said people should.

Jesus' teaching revolves around the idea of servanthood. Jesus refused the ordinary channels of worldly power and adopted what most people would call a lower-class lifestyle. In doing that, he revealed God's love, a love that works for the betterment of others rather than of oneself. Jesus truly was, as some have said, a "man for others."

In summing up the life of Jesus Christ, the most suitable word the apostle Paul could find was *servant* (Philippians 2:7). Actually, the Philippian text is much stronger, literally saying Jesus assumed the role of a slave. We know that in the first century slaves had virtually no rights. What a wonderful irony: Jesus became a slave in order that we might be free!

Holy Communion is the most powerful symbol for servanthood in the church's life. When the church gathers around the Lord's Table, we reenact Jesus' words at the Last Supper. Jesus told the disciples that they were partaking of his body and blood—his very life. By receiving that life, the disciples were identifying with it—and so do we when we receive the bread and cup. At Holy Communion we join the disciples in confessing our belief that both our life and the life of our nation can reach their potential when we share Jesus' life as servant to the world.

WORDS FOR MY LIFE

John Wesley, the founder of Methodism, believed and taught that God was especially close to Christians during Holy Communion. Wesley himself "communed" as many as ninety times a year, an average of once every four days!

Why did Wesley commune so much? He gives us the answer in his sermon "The Duty of Constant Communion." Wesley wrote that the benefits of Holy Communion are great. The benefits he experienced were "the forgiveness of past sins and the present strengthening and refreshing of our souls." With such blessings it is no wonder that Wesley received Holy Communion as often as he could.

Holy Communion meant a great deal to John Wesley and the early Methodists, but what does Holy Communion mean to us today? For Wesley, the elements of Communion (bread and cup) were "heavenly food." Are they heavenly food for us too? What happens when you and I receive the bread and cup? For Wesley, to receive Communion was at the same time to receive God's help. Do we have a sense of God's helping presence when we take Communion? For Wesley, the bread and cup conveyed God's mercy. Do we sense the mercy of God and the forgiveness of sins when we eat and drink the holy meal?

The early Methodists never rushed through their "sacramental meetings." Usually they would meet on Sunday afternoon and, depending on the size of the congregation, spend two or three hours in prayer, praise, and communing. They felt it was important not to hurry. Can you and I relate to this attitude? Are we excited on Communion Sundays? Do we believe God will be active in Communion? Do we anticipate a blessing? Are we willing to take time and not be rushed on Communion Sundays?

When Jesus broke the bread and passed the cup, he was sharing himself in a special but mysterious way. We should not be overly concerned, however, with how Christ comes to us in Holy Communion. Instead, we should be open to this divine sharing so we can become new persons in Christ. Holy Communion is one way God graces our lives so that we can really love God with all our hearts and love our neighbor as our very self.

18

Jesus Fulfills the Prophecy
Luke 4:16-30

The Spirit of the Lord is upon me,
because he has anointed me to preach
 good news to the poor.
He has sent me to proclaim release to
 the captives
and recovering of sight to the blind,
to set at liberty those who are oppressed,
to proclaim the acceptable year of the Lord.

Luke 4:18-19

WORDS FOR BIBLE TIMES

Jesus had been preaching throughout Galilee for almost a year (Luke 4:14-15) when he and his disciples turned toward Nazareth. This trip would be especially important since Jesus was well-known there. Nazareth was his home town. He had grown up there and learned the carpenter's trade. In the year he had been away, his fame had spread to every part of Galilee. The local people would be eager to hear him. Jesus had never preached in Nazareth before.

On the sabbath Jesus and his disciples went to the synagogue. Jesus often spoke in synagogues. The place was packed. Everyone expected Jesus to read a passage of Scripture and to interpret it. When the service came to the place where the writings of the prophets were read, Jesus stood up. He was given the Isaiah scroll. He carefully unrolled it until he found the passage he wanted: Isaiah

61:1-2. Then Jesus began to read Isaiah's description of the messiah who was to come. Everyone was quiet and still. When Jesus finished reading, he said, "Today this scripture has been fulfilled in your hearing" (Luke 4:21).

At first the people were amazed, many of them speaking well of Jesus. But then someone raised an objection: "Is not this Joseph's son?" (Luke 4:22). The mood in the synagogue began to change. How could Joseph's son be the Messiah? It was unthinkable! Jesus had gone too far this time. Then Jesus said, "Truly, I say to you, no prophet is acceptable in his own country" (Luke 4:24). The more Jesus spoke, the worse things got. Finally, filled with wrath, the men of the synagogue forced Jesus to go outside. They took him to a cliff, intending to throw him off and kill him. But Jesus calmly walked away and left Nazareth.

What was the message Jesus brought from Isaiah? The message was that he was the one of whom Isaiah spoke, the Messiah anointed by God's Spirit. Jesus also proclaimed that he was the embodiment of the good news to be preached to the poor.

Who are these poor? They include the destitute in spirit, being like prisoners of war who are dragged away by their conqueror, their own sins. These sins have thrown them into the inner dungeon, a place of darkness. There they are oppressed—crushed—by their desperate needs. To people like this Jesus brought release, sight, liberty! To such pitiful people Jesus proclaimed a year of Jubilee—God's acceptable time—a time of forgiveness, reconciliation, and peace.

What was true then is true now. Jesus Christ still brings the good news to all people.

WORDS FOR OUR TIME

Just before his ascension the risen Christ gave his disciples a mandate: "All authority in heaven and on earth has been given to me. Go therefore and make disciples of all nations, baptizing them in the name of the Father and of the Son and of the Holy Spirit, teaching them to observe all that I have commanded you; and lo, I am with you always, to the close of the age" (Matthew 28:18-20).

This mandate of Jesus is the foundation on which the church shapes its mission program. The church has accepted the task of bearing faithful witness to the nations of the world. And what is the content of this faithful witness? It is found in the Scripture for this lesson: Jesus is the anointed Messiah who brings the good news of God's salvation to a needy humanity.

Jesus' message to the synagogue at Nazareth has universal implications. While it is certainly true that Jesus preached his message first to the people of Israel, the Gentiles (non-Jews) are also included in God's vast redemptive plan. In fact, we see the beginnings of the church's mission work among Gentiles as early as Peter's witness to Cornelius the centurion (Acts 10:1-43). As we learn from John 3:16, God's love for everyone in the world prompted the sending of Christ.

In one way or another every reader of this lesson is the product of Christian missions. For example, many of us can trace our ancestry all the way back to northern European tribes. Our ancient ancestors were a savage, barbarian people who lived largely in the forests. The good news of God's redemptive love came to them through the faithful work of Christian missionaries. As a result of their labors, our ancestors gradually turned to Christ. Love replaced hatred, and peacefulness replaced war in their hearts. Today we benefit from the work of those missionaries. This same story can be told in regard to each of us, regardless of who we are and where we are from.

Jesus Christ has fulfilled the ancient prophecies and has brought saving love into human history. This glorious good news fills Christians with joy. As a result of this joy Christians continue to pray for and support the mission endeavors of the church. We know the love of Christ can be effective in the lives of all people, whether they live down the street or at the farthest corner of the earth. Christ still brings release, sight, and liberty to those oppressed by sin and circumstance. Alleluia!

WORDS FOR MY LIFE

Talk about mixed emotions! Think about what Jesus faced in that synagogue in Nazareth. At first the people were curious about and interested in Jesus. They listened eagerly. Their first response to him was delight. They were happy with what he said. They admired him. Then someone raised an objection, and doubt fell on the group. When Jesus said a prophet is not honored in his own country, the people were offended. Luke 4:28 says they were "filled with wrath." Those who were satisfied with him only a few moments before were now ready to murder him! It is no wonder that, as far as we know, Jesus never preached again in Nazareth.

Why did the people object to what Jesus said? They understood perfectly well what he meant. Using Isaiah 61:1-2 as his text, Jesus told them he was the Anointed One from God who could release them from their sins and open their spiritually blind eyes. Was this not the good news for which they had been waiting so long? It was, but these people did not want to hear it from Jesus. You see, they were willing to think highly of Jesus. They were willing to accept him as an unusually gifted teacher. In fact, they would even honor him with the title *prophet.* But to say he was the Messiah—no way! After all, wasn't he just Joseph's son?

Look at these worshipers a minute. They were probably just like you and me. They wanted to worship God and to follow God's ways. They were as faithful to the law as they could be. This is the frightening part of this whole account: Good people—worshipers of God—became filled with a killer instinct. Is it possible that we too praise Jesus one minute and turn on him the next? Do we turn away from Christ if his teachings get too close to where we live? Do the members of that congregation make up a mirror in which you see your own reflection?

19

The Good Samaritan
Luke 10:25-37

You shall love the Lord your God with all your heart, and with all your soul, and with all your strength, and with all your mind; and your neighbor as yourself.

Luke 10:27

WORDS FOR BIBLE TIMES

Jesus loved using parables as ways to teach truths about God. Parables were short stories designed to compare someone in the parable with someone listening to it. In fact, the word *parable* means comparison. Jesus' parables were not always appreciated because many of them were stinging rebukes of those who listened. The parable we are about to study was so shocking to the people who heard it that it must have seemed scandalous to them.

The parable of the good Samaritan is one of Jesus' better-known parables. Ironically, it is also one of the least understood. Many people think of this story as an ethical teaching on how to be a good neighbor. Actually, this is a theological parable, responding to a clever lawyer's question, "What shall I do to inherit eternal life?" (Luke 10:25).

Jesus does not answer the lawyer directly but asks another question instead: "What is written in the law? How do you read?" (Luke 10:26). The lawyer responds by combining two commandments: Love God with all your heart (Deuteronomy 6:5) and your neighbor as yourself (Leviticus 19:18). "You have answered right," remarks Jesus; "do this, and you will live" (Luke 10:28).

But seeking "to justify himself," the lawyer asks, "Who is my neighbor?" (Luke 10:29). The lawyer apparently expected Jesus to respond by giving him a list of those he was to think of as his neighbors. Instead, Jesus tells a parable, a parable about robbers who beat a man nearly to death, about a priest and a Levite who refuse to render aid, about a Samaritan—a member of a people hated by those who lived in Judea—who goes the second mile in caring for the needs of the unconscious victim.

In the parable the question "Who is my neighbor?" becomes "To whom must I become a neighbor?" The obvious answer is to any person in need, even to an enemy. True love turns into compassion for anyone who hurts. And what is the source of such love? Such love can only come from God. Therefore, whoever loves with such love inherits eternal life. Why? Because the love of God that motivates such selfless compassion is the love that results in eternal life. The lawyer must rise above the popular prejudices of his people against Samaritans, heretics, traitors, and Gentiles.

The lawyer had tried to trick Jesus. But he was unable to do so and then tried to save face before the group. The Bible does not tell us how the lawyer responded to the parable. What do you think? Was the love of God too costly for him?

WORDS FOR OUR TIME

Jesus' teaching on the equality of persons, regardless of skin color, nationality, or speech pattern, cut deeply into the prevailing mood of his day. As far as the Romans were concerned, if you were not a Roman, you were a barbarian. As far as the Jews were concerned, they were the chosen people. The rest were Gentiles. As Jews they had been taught to care for their own and to avoid contact with sinners.

This kind of attitude furnished part of the justification for the actions of the priest and the Levite in the parable.

The beaten man was unconscious and naked. No one could tell whether he was a Jew or a Gentile. If he was a Gentile and the priest and the Levite touched him, that would pose serious problems of ritual purification for them. Better not to get involved. That seemed best.

"To whom must I become a neighbor?" is a question for our world just as much as it was for the people in Jesus' parable. From our infancy we too are taught, directly and indirectly, that some people are better, worthier, than others. We become fearful of those who are different, and we look down on them as a way of attempting to control them. We often limit the idea of neighbor to "our" group of relatives and associates.

Prejudice effectively blocks compassion, and every person who hurts deserves Christian compassion. Didn't Jesus say, "You have heard that it was said, 'You shall love your neighbor and hate your enemy.' But I say to you, Love your enemies and pray for those who persecute you, so that you may be sons of your Father who is in heaven" (Matthew 5:43-45).

How are some people segregated or discriminated against in your city or town? In what ways does your church reach out to these people with the love of Jesus? What kind of strategies does your church need to develop in order to become compassionate toward and to help the poor and oppressed?

WORDS FOR MY LIFE

Jesus fully identified with us in order to bring us the gift of salvation. Paul says Jesus took on himself the lowest form of existence, a slave (Philippians 2:7). The writer of Hebrews says Jesus "has suffered and been tempted" just as we suffer and are tempted (Hebrews 2:18). Jesus has compassion on us because he was one of us. Jesus knows our needs. Therefore, nothing can separate us from God's love (Romans 8:38-39).

When the lawyer quizzed Jesus with the question, "What shall I do to inherit eternal life?" (Luke 10:25), he expected Jesus to give him a list of "do's" and "don'ts."

But Jesus was concerned with "being"—who the lawyer was in the depths of his heart. Sometimes we think being a Christian means following a list of "do's" and "don'ts." But Jesus Christ is first of all concerned with our hearts. He knows that if we are what we are supposed to be, we will do what we are supposed to do.

The beauty of the Samaritan is that his compassion destroyed any potential barrier between him and the wounded man. The Samaritan can represent that person so changed by God's grace that a new life—a new attitude— comes into existence. People who will receive eternal life are those whose very "being" has been changed by God. Such people have taken on the love and compassion of Jesus.

The parable reminds us that one proof of our life in Christ is that we see others differently from the way we used to see them. People become opportunities for compassionate care rather than objects for competition. And this compassion, this identification with the hurts and dilemmas of others, becomes a natural response. Christians do not decide to be compassionate. Christians are naturally compassionate.

Jesus Christ has taught us to be open to others and not to prejudge them. We are even to give our enemies the benefit of the doubt by praying for them and by being kind to them. Christians are indeed radically different people, as Peter remarked (1 Peter 2:9-10). To self-righteous persons who always compare themselves to others, the good Samaritan will always appear as a disturber.

How should we react to the parable of the good Samaritan? We could ask ourselves if we find joy in serving others without feeling we have to control them. Do we consider ourselves to be totally dependent on God's grace for our life now and hereafter? Do we give up positions or attitudes of power in order to reach out as a brother or sister to those who are the poor of our society? Do we want to be identified with the good Samaritan?

20

The Waiting Father
Luke 15:11-32

While he was yet at a distance, his father saw him and had compassion, and ran and embraced him and kissed him.

Luke 15:20

WORDS FOR BIBLE TIMES

In the Middle East it was (and still is) an honor to be invited to someone's house for a meal. Such an invitation was an offer of peace, friendship, and trust. When Jesus ate with "sinners" (Luke 15:1-2), he gave evidence of his saving ministry. Jesus steadfastly refused to exclude anyone from God's love. However, as the Gospel of Luke shows, Jesus' loving association with sinners, or unclean people, was an affront to some religious authorities (Luke 5:27-32; 7:36-50).

The fifteenth chapter of Luke contains three of Jesus' parables. They have a common theme: revealing the mercy of God to all people. The third and longest parable is about a father and two sons. The father is the focus of the story. The two sons in a sense are symbols of Gentiles and Jews respectively. This parable is often called the parable of the prodigal son. But the deeper we enter into the parable, the more we see it as a parable of the waiting father.

This parable is unusually rich in meaning. The two sons act in two entirely different ways. The first gets fed up with life at home, demands his inheritance (while his father is still alive), and heads for what he believes will be fun and fortune. He falls on desperate times, to the point of almost starving. Thinking of the comforts of home, he decides to return there and try to hire out to his father as a menial laborer. But much to his surprise his father runs to meet him, clothes him in luxurious garments, and throws a marvelous feast for rejoicing. The son truly repents and is reinstated as a full family member. Thus the one (the Gentile) who was outside (the covenant) was completely restored (forgiven and accepted).

The second son is bitter and jealous. He angrily rails against his brother and humiliates his father. The ingratitude of this son is staggering, according to Middle Eastern custom. He has already refused to follow tradition and act as a reconciler between the father and the first son. Now he would rather not have his brother home. The father lovingly reminds the angry brother of his privileges. In contrast to the first son, with this son the story comes to no conclusion. The older son (representing the religious authorities), who was inside (the covenant), also rebelled. His fate was in the hands of those who heard the parable. The open question is, Will the religious authorities repent?

The father is a study in himself. He breaks custom by not punishing either son. He accepts their insults, an unbelievable act in Middle Eastern culture. He welcomes the younger son and tries to win over the older. The father is completely self-giving, eager to forgive, and lavish in his gifts (of salvation). He does not want either son (Gentile or Jew) to be lost, though he will not force them to be obedient. A more marvelous portrait of God cannot be found in the Bible!

WORDS FOR OUR TIME

While running for office, President Bush expressed his desire that America become a kinder and gentler nation. He promised to work toward such a high ideal if elected. With that wish he touched a responsive cord in many people. The hope for more kindness in our relationships and for gentleness in our dealings appeals to all of us, regardless of our political persuasion. Christians especially hope that all elected officials will spend their energies working for peace, tranquility, and good will at home and abroad.

The church is attracted to sensitivities like those President Bush spoke of because it sees them as extensions of the character of God. Christians believe that God is kind, gentle, patient, and caring. The Bible repeatedly announces God's deep desire to share God's character with us, to the extent that we become images of the greatness of the love of God. Such is the portrait of God Jesus draws in the parable of the waiting father.

How we yearn for this love in our families, on the job, and among all our personal contacts. Instinctively, we know life would be richer and fuller if we could experience such love. But everywhere barriers are erected against it, barriers like self-interest, party spirit, and anger. Is such love impossible for us? No! says the parable.

God wants to share love. In fact, the way we know that God is love is that God shares love with us! The love of God is relational. We know the character of the father in the parable by the way he relates to his sons. Love cannot be merely a private affair. True love is social. God is love because God attempts to share kindness, gentleness, patience, and caring with us. The parable calls us to open ourselves to this incredible love. If we do, we will find life changing for the good all around us.

WORDS FOR MY LIFE

Those who heard Jesus tell the parable of the waiting father knew he was calling them to make a decision. This decision was direct and quite personal. Jesus was calling the people to repent and return to God. The only question was, Would they do it? Would the elder son accept the unquestioning love of the father? Would the whole family be restored to such a caring father? If you were the elder son, what would you do?

The people to whom Jesus was speaking were well informed about their religious past. But over the years they had allowed the spiritual tradition of Israel to be codified as laws. In doing so, they lost "the spirit" of the law, which was the most important thing. Jesus called the people "to turn" (repent), to change their minds. Jesus wanted them to turn from the frozen rigidity of the law to the living God. *Repentance* was therefore a gracious word but one hard to accept.

Why is it so difficult to admit our sins? Why did the elder son react so stubbornly to the gracious words of his father? Perhaps if we look at the possible motives of the elder son, we will better understand ourselves and others.

What do you think? Did the elder son reject his father's overtures because he was

(1) too proud;
(2) overcome with jealousy at the way the younger son was treated;
(3) fearful of what might happen if he gave control of his life to his father?

What motive could be strong enough to cause this son to be so hostile toward his father and brother? The confused anger of the elder son should arouse our pity. He totally missed the point of his father's patience and graciousness.

The message of this parable is as fresh today as it was in the first century. Jesus stills calls people, inside and outside the church, to repent when they do not have "the spirit" of true faith.

The real tragedy is that Jesus' hearers did not believe they needed to repent. *Why is he speaking this way to us?* they must have thought. After all, they considered themselves to be "the right kind of people." But good words and a good reputation are deadly when they become substitutes for living faith. Is it possible today for baptism, church attendance, and good works to become barriers to hearing the gracious voice of God?

Knowing the ever-present danger of misguided religiosity, the apostle Paul urged the Corinthians to "examine yourselves, to see whether you are holding to your faith" (2 Corinthians 13:5). If you examine yourself honestly, which son represents the true direction of your life?

21
The Coming of the Word
John 1:1-18

The Word became flesh and dwelt among us, full of grace and truth; we have beheld his glory, glory as of the only Son from the Father.

John 1:14

WORDS FOR BIBLE TIMES

John's Gospel is unique among the four Gospels of the New Testament. Matthew, Mark, and Luke are basically narratives of Jesus' ministry. On the other hand, the Gospel of John records only twenty-one days of Jesus' life. Those "days" are so arranged as to meet the author's purpose for writing: "These are written that you may believe that Jesus is the Christ, the Son of God, and that believing you may have life in his name" (John 20:31). John's Gospel is therefore evangelistic as well as theological.

John begins his Gospel with a "hymn" to the Word (John 1:1-18). The printed text above contains the central thought of the hymn. This hymn serves as an introduction to the Gospel. The hymn contains quite lofty language, so lofty that commentators strain to find adequate ways to interpret it for us. We stand in awe before John's marvelous tribute to Jesus Christ, the bringer of life and light.

This hymn has four stanzas, in which are intermixed comments by the writer. The hymn is beautiful, beginning in the heavens and ending on earth. Let us look at the hymn.

Stanza 1 (verses 1-2): "The Word Is Praised"

Before there were worlds or galaxies, the Word existed.
The Word is like God, eternal in nature, because the
Word is God. At the same time, it can be said that the
Word existed alongside God. This point is pure mystery!
The opening words of this hymn are the same as in the
opening of the Book of Genesis: "In the beginning."
These are words that speak of eternity—of a quality of
being.

Stanza 2 (verses 3-5): "The Word Creates"

This stanza contains a deliberate parallel to the account
of Creation in Genesis 1. The Word is responsible for
creating more than trees or animals; the Word creates
"life." This life, a pattern of the divine, is also "light"
(insight, recognition). The light the Word reveals shines
in the darkness (the reality of evil), offering hope in place
of despair and ruin.

Stanza 3 (verses 10-12): "The Word Comes to the World"

The Word, the essence of God, becomes incarnate in
human flesh and is thereby manifested to the world. But
the world rejects (does not accept) the light-bearing Word.
Darkness seems generally to prevail. Some persons recognize the Word, however, and are thereby empowered to
become God's children. Verses 6-9 tell us the Word is
Jesus Christ.

*Stanza 4 (verses 14 and 16): "The Word Among the
Faithful"*

The community of faith beheld the Word that had
become flesh. This Word lived on earth for a short while.
The Word has shown his "glory" (visible brightness), the
glory of enduring love. And this fullness of love is shared
in the community of faith. Praise to the faithful Word!
Praise to Jesus Christ!

WORDS FOR OUR TIME

The major theme of our Scripture passage is that the
divine Word took on flesh and ministers to the world. By
ministry we mean that the Word (the full expression of
God) brings light and life to people. Acceptance of this

heavenly Word creates a community of faith. This community of the Word lives in the divine love coming through Jesus Christ, who is the Word.

John's assumption is that the world largely lacks the good qualities Jesus brings: light, life, and love. We need to realize that Jesus, as God's Word, does not simply enhance our lives. No, Jesus changes our lives by the gifts he brings. Once we lived in "darkness"; but by accepting him, we begin to live his life and to share in his light and love. We see that John presents darkness and light as two basic attitudes toward life.

When John writes of God's light overcoming the world's darkness, he is not thinking of a gentle dawn slowly displacing the dark of night. Not at all! The light is more like a lightning flash in the midst of a terrible storm. Darkness is much more than the mere absence of light. Darkness is an active attitude or force, a way of living that thrives on deception, hatred, and death. When the Word engages the darkness in us, it is like the clashing of swords and the sound of battle.

What evidence of darkness do you see in your community? in American society? in the world? How can your church help bring the true light of life and love to the world?

WORDS FOR MY LIFE

The Gospel writer John is often portrayed in religious symbolism as an eagle. Just as this majestic bird soars through the heights, so John, as suggested by our text, soars in the heady atmosphere of divine mystery. If we would grasp the meaning of John's Gospel, especially the "hymn to the Word," we must look beyond ordinary ways of understanding and enter into a relationship with the Word.

What does it mean to enter into a relationship with the Word? It means to "believe" in the Word. Over ninety times in his Gospel, John calls you and me to believe. Believing is much more than saying, "Oh yes, I believe in the Christ of the church's creeds," however. Authentic belief is to trust Christ so deeply that we shape our lives according to his teaching. To accept the good news of Jesus and to live by his sayings is to receive God's "power" (or authority); it is to be "born" a child of God (John 1:12-13).

To come to genuine belief in Jesus as the Christ may take a long time, or it may come as a sudden flash of insight.

Ruth was a gracious lady and the organist of the church I served as an assistant to the minister. Once a week I went to her house at noon for a piano lesson and a bite of lunch. We always talked about the work of the church, especially its evangelistic outreach.

One sun-drenched day I went to Ruth's house as usual. After knocking at the door, I hear a muffled voice say, "Come in." I walked in. Ruth was in the kitchen, stirring something in a pot and crying. "Ruth, what's wrong?" I asked. "It's on the table," was all she could say.

I expected to see a telegram telling of the death of her father-in-law, who suffered from heart disease. But all I saw was an open Sunday school book. "I don't see anything on the table," I said. "Read it," she replied. "Read it out loud." Picking up the book, I read the printed text for the lesson. It was the story of Jesus' death.

When I finished, Ruth said, "He really did it! He really did it!" The deep truth of the mystery of Jesus Christ's death had dawned on her in a new and personal way. She had come to real belief in Christ. The Word had come to her. The divine mystery was alive in her heart. We did not eat much lunch that day, and there was no piano lesson! But the two of us did a lot of celebrating.

John writes that Jesus (the Word) was "full of grace and truth. . . . And from his fulness have we all received, grace upon grace" (John 1:14, 16). The Word came into the world in order that we might experience God's saving grace. The Word came to reveal God to seeking hearts (John 1:17-18). The question is, have we, like Ruth, opened our hearts to the mystery that is Christ? Has the Word come alive in our hearts too? Do we really believe?

22

The Good Shepherd
John 10:1-18

I am the good shepherd; I know my own and my own know me.

John 10:14

WORDS FOR BIBLE TIMES

It was near the end of Jesus' public ministry, John tells us, when Jesus attended the annual Feast of Tabernacles in Jerusalem (John 7:2, 10). A week-long celebration, the Feast of Tabernacles marked the conclusion of the harvest season. Usually the air was filled with prayers of thanksgiving, but this year there was a different mood. Jesus was teaching and healing in the Temple precincts, and John says the people were divided over what he said. Opposition to Jesus was especially intense among the religious authorities because they sensed his challenge to their power over the people.

"I am the door," said Jesus (John 10:7). "I am the good shepherd" (John 10:11). The stories of the door of the sheepfold and the good shepherd are parables. The biblical text reports that Jesus told them just after he healed a man who had been blind from birth (John 9). Instead of being happy that a man had been healed, the religious authorities were angry that the healing had taken place on the sabbath. In response to their reactions Jesus told the parables of the door of the sheepfold and the good shepherd.

In pastoral language Jesus drew sharp distinctions between himself and the religious leaders. But they did not understand. That is reflected in their critical reactions to him (John 10:19-21).

Jesus used three primary metaphors to get his message across. First, he said that he is the only door (or gate) leading into the protective sheepfold (John 10:1-3a). Others, religious leaders with their warped view of the law, not only failed to be doors opening to the sheepfold, they were thieves and robbers.

Second, Jesus said that he is the good shepherd who cares for and protects the sheep (John 10:3b-4). He alone is capable of leading the sheep to abundant pastures (real life). Others only pretended to be shepherds. When danger came (the wolf), they would run away as fast as they could, leaving the sheep exposed and in trouble.

Third, Jesus said that the people (the sheep) recognized and accepted him (John 10:4-5). Like the blind man in John 9, the people would instinctively know they could trust him. In this parable acceptance of Jesus meant rejection of the supposed authority of the religious leaders. Thus what Jesus said provoked a crisis of faith among the people. The leaders failed to be aware of this situation, caught up as they were with their own position. For them Jesus' words were simply a threat to their power.

WORDS FOR OUR TIME

The words of Jesus about being a "good shepherd" for us convey a sense of protection, security, and rest. In many ways Jesus' words here remind us of Psalm 23. The idea of Jesus as good shepherd must speak of caring leadership, of hope instead of despair.

Yet there is another, more radical, message in John 10:1-18. At first glance this marvelous teaching of Jesus as good shepherd may appear somewhat tame and even tranquil. But in its social and religious setting it hid an announcement that was powerful and disruptive.

For the prophet Isaiah the shepherding care of God is combined with God as warrior-ruler (Isaiah 40:10-11). When one speaks of God or Jesus as shepherd, a particular kind of shepherd is meant. The shepherd is kind to the sheep, leading them to pasture with the call of his soothing voice. But to the wolf the shepherd is eternal foe and does not hesitate to throw himself between the sheep and this vicious danger. Likewise to the downtrodden, the poor, and the maimed, Jesus comes as teacher and healer; but to power manipulators, he comes as divine judge.

When Jesus announces that he alone is the good shepherd, he is, in effect, drawing a line in the sand. Although this announcement was good news to the brokenhearted and penniless, it was bad news to religious leaders who sanctioned the status quo. Jesus discredited the religious interests and authority of the religious leaders who opposed him. That they understood his threat to their power is clear from their reactions: accusing him of being possessed by demons (insane).

For us this message is that security and meaning in life can only be found in Jesus. All governmental programs, social engineering, and international maneuvering are ultimately doomed. The kingdom of peace has been announced by Jesus and must be brought by Jesus. Christians are those people who live out the risk of aligning their lives with the life and teachings of Jesus.

How can Christians be responsible to a society they sense is self-defeating? How can the church maintain its fidelity to God's will when it is under constant social pressure to conform? How can Christians best bear witness to the message of the Kingdom and its demands?

WORDS FOR MY LIFE

John 10:1-18 is primarily concerned with the uniqueness of Jesus' ministry and character. The sheep—the people—are hardly mentioned, either corporately or individually. Yet there is enough information about those who follow Jesus to enable me to make four statements.

(1) *Jesus is the door through which I am permitted to enter into real life.* Jesus said, "I am the door; if any one enters by me, he will be saved, and will go in and out and find pasture" (John 10:9). The pasture is a symbol for abundant life (John 10:10). The writer wants you and me to know that Jesus is the way to the fullness of the kingdom of God (John 20:31).

(2) *Jesus is a loving caregiver who knows me personally.*
Jesus said, "I am the good shepherd; I know my own and
my own know me" (John 10:14). Because we are part of
Jesus' flock, we can recognize his voice. Properly sensi-
tized, we will not follow a stranger, trusting as we do only
in the true shepherd (John 10:4-5). The United Methodist
tradition teaches that the Holy Spirit draws us to Jesus and
enables us to discern his voice in our hearts. This teaching
is affirmed by Romans 8:14-17, where Paul tells us the
Spirit establishes an intimate relationship between God
and us.

(3) *Jesus actively protects me from being overwhelmed by
evil.* Evil is like a savage wolf that would maim and kill
the flock of God if it could. "The good shepherd," Jesus
said, "lays down his life for the sheep" (John 10:11). This
statement is a major teaching of this passage of Scripture.
Jesus says he freely lays his life down for us (John 10:15,
17-18). In a way essentially unknown to us, Jesus Christ
protects us against the onslaught of the wolf, the deceptive
voice of strangers, and the wicked intentions of thieves
and robbers. The death of the shepherd keeps the sheep
from dying.

Paradoxically, the Bible teaches that the Christian life is
often one of suffering. Yet we can confidently claim in the
midst of our deepest trials that God's love helps and
protects us (1 Corinthians 10:13).

(4) *Jesus makes me a member of a worldwide family.* "I
have other sheep," Jesus said, "that are not of this fold; I
must bring them also, and they will heed my voice. So
there shall be one flock, one shepherd" (John 10:16).
Scholars understand Jesus to be referring to Gentile as well
as to Jewish believers. Everyone can be included in the
secure flock of God! The universal church is our home,
and its members are our sisters and brothers.

How does it make you feel to know that Jesus desires to
lead you into real life? Are you glad Jesus knows you
personally? How can Jesus help you bear the weight of
temptation and evil? How is your attitude toward the
church changed by thinking of it as the flock of God?

23

The Day of Pentecost
Acts 2:1-36

In the last days it shall be, God declares,
that I will pour out my Spirit upon all flesh.

Acts 2:17

WORDS FOR BIBLE TIMES

The church is richer indeed because Luke, disciple of
Jesus and friend of Paul, was a historian as well as a
physician. The Gospel he wrote is full of joy and singing,
especially in the early chapters that deal with Jesus' birth
and childhood. The Book of Acts, Luke's sequel to his
Gospel, continues the story of Jesus. Acts begins with joy
and excitement in the account of the day of Pentecost.
No other New Testament writer gives us such a compre-
hensive view of the good news of Jesus turned loose in the
world.

The explosive second chapter sets the tone of the Book
of Acts by describing the coming of the Holy Spirit. These
forty-seven verses report the Spirit's descent, Peter's sermon and its meaning, and the birth of a new community
of faith. The remaining chapters of the Book of Acts give
an overview of thirty-three years of early church history, a
history filled with the Spirit and fired with bold witnesses.
The story of our heritage is stirring and dramatic.

Luke tells us that the disciples and other believers
gathered in an upper room in Jerusalem to pray together
and to wait for the promised Spirit of God (Acts 1:8,
12-14). Early in the morning of the first day of the Feast
of Pentecost, the Holy Spirit descended on the tiny group.

A tremendous sound like a windstorm filled the room, and something like tongues of fire was seen above these persons' heads. Unable to contain their excitement, the disciples spilled out into the streets and told passers-by what was happening. Not expecting such a rush of enthusiasm, the people did not know what to make of all this. Some even thought the disciples were drunk! But what amazed the people most was that the disciples were able to speak with them in their native language about the living Christ.

Then Peter, spokesperson for the disciples, lifted his voice and called for calm. Everyone grew quiet. Peter began to preach (Acts 2:14-36). His sermon was so powerful that it has been considered ever since to be the time when the church as an organization was born. Peter preached of the beauty of the Lord: Christ died, Christ rose, Christ was exalted.

"Listen everyone," he said. "It's too early in the morning for these people to be drunk. What you see and hear is nothing less than the fulfillment of what the prophet says. The Spirit will be poured out on the people of God before the Day of Judgment comes (Joel 2:28-32). And Joel's prophecy relates to the ministry of Jesus Christ, who has been raised from the dead by the power of God."

Peter went on to say, "Even King David testifies that God did not abandon the Messiah to the grave (Psalm 16:8-11). No. Rather, God raised up Jesus, who has now poured out the Holy Spirit on us. The Lord is now exalted, as you can plainly read in Psalm 110:1. You see, God has made Jesus both Lord and Christ!"

The descent of the Spirit produced great joy and bold preaching. Many people believed Peter's inspired message, and a community of faith was formed. The church was born! Christian mission was beginning!

WORDS FOR OUR TIME

To read of the exploits of the early church is quite moving. Our own faith is kindled as we relive the fearless witness and desperate trials of our spiritual parents. A rush of spiritual energy and singleness of purpose gripped the church. By comparison our lives may seem tame. Enthusiasm within the church may seem cool today. At times we seem only a pale reflection of our Christian past.

How we Christians interpret the Book of Acts is crucial for our self-understanding. But as we read about the Spirit of Pentecost, we must ask ourselves some painful questions. For example, do we have a tendency to withdraw from society, feeling overwhelmed and powerless to cope with its demands? Do we seem to be competitors with other groups of Christians rather than happy family members? Who is "on the run" in our communities, the church or the forces of evil? Do we seek the blessings of Pentecost without its obligations?

The Spirit of Pentecost is a recreating, correcting Spirit. Where the church is experiencing the Spirit, we see Christians involved in both worship and social change. What evil has broken apart, the Spirit of Pentecost is able to put back together. To illustrate this principle, scholars see a connection between the story of the tower of Babel and the Pentecostal gift of understanding.

In Genesis 11:1-9, we read that because of pride people lost the ability to communicate with one another. Lacking a common language, people became separated from one another; and they lost their love and respect for God. This radical division between peoples lasted until Pentecost. On Pentecost the Spirit of God gave gifts of understanding that brought people together in community and praise. Social and religious barriers were overcome as the Holy Spirit recreated people into one family in God. And wherever and whenever people are aware of the presence of the Spirit of the Lord, this kind of healing, reconciling work continues; and the forces of evil are brought up short!

WORDS FOR MY LIFE

Pentecost was a continuation of the life-changing good news of Jesus Christ. The message of Pentecost was of the nearness of God. This message brought the assurance that God is love and that the Christian faith is real and true.

When the Spirit of Pentecost fills our hearts, we find this blessed assurance happening all over again.

The witnessing, in-filling Spirit is a type of new incarnation. The active love of Jesus continues in the church through the Spirit. And when the church is filled with the Spirit, the gospel is offered as a vital force for people's lives. The remembrance of the first Pentecost is a kind of promise that the same Spirit can come with power to you and me. This is really good news, isn't it?

If we are to experience the Spirit in our lives, what are we to expect? What are we to look for? Are we to anticipate that we will hear a mighty sound from heaven? Will we see tongues of fire above the heads of believers? Will we be able to speak in languages we have never learned? The church has been cautious at this point, emphasizing that the important thing is the Spirit, not the manifestations of the Spirit's presence. But can we be too cautious and perhaps miss the time of the Spirit with us?

If we take the day of Pentecost as our guide, we can safely know when the Holy Spirit is filling our lives. How? First, the Spirit comes to those who seek the presence of Christ through prayer and waiting. The Spirit will not be rushed. As we wait in utter dependence on God, we can expect God to send the Spirit to us at the appropriate time.

Second, when the Spirit comes, Christians are filled with a desire to share their faith. With this desire comes a certain loving boldness to witness. The apostle Peter is a prime example. Whereas he was once intimidated by a maid after Jesus' arrest, now he speaks forthrightly and without regard to the consequences.

Third, the Spirit bound the early Christians together in a common bond of love and obedience. We can be sure the Spirit has come when we genuinely love other Christians, regardless of their distinctiveness.

Finally, the Spirit is moving when God's people are filled with joy. To know Christ is glorious! The Spirit releases praise among the people of God, and this fact accounts for the excitement the first Christians felt.

Now the question becomes, Is the Holy Spirit filling your heart with the blessings of Pentecost?

24

The Mind of Christ
Philippians 2:1-11

Have this mind among yourselves, which is yours in Christ Jesus.

Philippians 2:5

WORDS FOR BIBLE TIMES

The apostle Paul had preached the gospel for more than twenty years when he wrote his stirring letter to the Philippians. Paul had suffered much as an evangelist. Now he was under house arrest, probably in Caesarea, waiting trial because of his witness to Christ. Unable to travel, the apostle wrote letters of encouragement to various congregations. Of those letters none is more personal, more appreciative, or more joyous than his letter to the Philippians.

The Philippian church had been especially close to Paul, supporting his ministry in many ways. He was grateful for the love of these Christians. Yet that love seemed to be missing in their relationships with one another. That is, for reasons we do not know, the Philippian Christians were taking sides against one another. Paul sensed that one of the desperate needs of the congregation was unity. The biblical text for this lesson picks up the apostle's concern that the Philippian Christians be one in spirit, one in zeal, and one in purpose.

Philippians 2:1-11 divides into two sections. First we read of Paul teaching that Christian unity is based on humility and self-sacrifice. He begins by calling attention to the blessings God had given the Philippians: human encouragement and consolation, the fellowship of the Holy

Spirit, and God's own affection and compassion (Philippians 2:1). With so many good things in their lives, Paul says his joy will be complete if they will just be one in mind, heart, zeal, and purpose (Philippians 2:2).

A principle of spiritual growth is that good attitudes must replace bad ones. So Paul told the Philippians that something in them had to go. That something was a spirit of rivalry (Philippians 2:3). From the context we understand Paul to be warning the Philippians about (1) fighting for an idea they think is right even when it is actually wrong and (2) selfishly looking out for their own individual interests without regard for the interests of others. So what is the antidote to rivalry? The antidote is loving one another unselfishly (Philippians 2:4). This is the way to achieve Christian community: to consider others as better than ourselves.

The second section of our text is an example Paul gives of what it means to have unity through humility and self-sacrifice. The apostle chooses Jesus himself as the church's model. Paul's use of Christ as an example can be divided into two parts: (1) Look what Christ did! and (2) Look what God did!

What did Christ do? He willingly set aside his special rights as God's Son, accepted public humiliation, and obeyed God to the extent of accepting death on the cross (Philippians 2:6-8). The Philippians, Paul writes, are to have this same spirit about themselves.

And what did God do? God exalted Jesus at the appropriate time, giving him the name *Lord* (Philippians 2:10-11). The message is clear: If we humble ourselves and serve one another, God will do the exalting; and God will do so in God's own time.

WORDS FOR OUR TIME

Low self-esteem is a chronic problem among people today. Most of us seem to suffer from feelings of inferiority and inadequacy of one kind or another. Compulsively driven people, such as workaholics, have high needs to achieve, to be somebody, to ward off feelings of unworthiness. In a biography a motion picture actress lamented how unsure she was of her performances, even if others liked them. She was severely apprehensive about professional reviews. In spite of her public image as one who was secure and in charge, she was nervous and often afraid. She wanted to please people and was constantly worried about failing. One thing all of us want these days is to feel good about ourselves, to know ourselves as persons of worth. Like the actress, we know that is easier said than done!

The church is sometimes blamed for perpetuating feelings of guilt and poor self-esteem. A student in a graduate class I was teaching, herself a secondary school teacher, lashed out in anger against the church. "All the church does is create false guilt," she said, "and then expect people to pay it money to get rid of it!"

We must admit that the church has at times taught that the body is bad, that deep feelings, especially sexual ones, are forbidden, and that persons need to be stripped of any sense of ego. But when Paul speaks of humility, he does not mean being without personal rights or denying oneself pleasure or considering oneself to be a totally worthless person. Paul's supreme example of humility was Jesus, who exercised his rights at times, enjoyed pleasurable occasions, and had a healthy view of himself. True humility and self-sacrifice follow when we value others as persons of worth, as deserving to be appreciated and loved, and as deserving to be treated with the utmost respect.

Paul's concern is an ethical one. The question is how Christians are to treat one another. Of course, there is a spillover effect onto society at large. Christians are not only to love their own but everyone else as well. The church certainly ought to be one place where an apprehensive person feels secure, where a guilty person feels accepted and forgiven, and where a broken person feels healed.

WORDS FOR MY LIFE

All Christians know that Jesus Christ is *Savior* in the most complete sense of that word. Paul feels it necessary, however, to remind the Philippians—and us—that their primary task is to follow Jesus' teachings and way of life. In his comments Paul says Jesus is to be our model in both humility and obedience.

The humility of Christ: Jesus once characterized himself by saying, "I am gentle and lowly in heart" (Matthew 11:29). That is, Jesus was content with the privilege of serving others. In the Sermon on the Mount he urged his listeners to be meek in spirit (Matthew 5:5). By that he meant that they were to accept God's way rather than demanding their own way. The notion of humility as listening to God is the main idea behind Philippians 2:8.

To follow Jesus in humility means we are to follow God's will for our lives joyously. We are to esteem others highly and to count as valuable any service we can render them (Philippians 2:3-4). Humility means we look to Christ for our sense of self-worth.

The obedience of Christ: Humility of spirit enabled Jesus to accept the cross obediently (Philippians 2:8). In the garden of Gethsemane he prayed, "Not what I will, but what thou wilt" (Mark 14:36). This kind of deference to God was seen in Jesus calling God "Father." Jesus' desire to be obedient to God was tested early in his ministry. The temptations in the wilderness (Matthew 4:1-11) showed Jesus' determination to do only God's will (see also John 4:34; 5:30; 8:29; 17:4).

To follow Jesus in obedience means to recognize that we need God if we are to know who we are and if we are to lead a worthwhile life. To follow Jesus means we are to trust God, knowing in our hearts that whatever God prepares for us is best. Finally, it means that we are to embrace suffering if that is the price of our Christian witness.

The Christian life is often a rugged affair. Being a Christian calls for resignation to God's will and determined following of Christ. At the same time, being a Christian requires us to recognize that we cannot go it alone. We must have God's grace and guidance. Living as a Christian at the end of the twentieth century means that we are to be open to God's leading as we walk through a largely uncharted way. Living as a Christian also means recognizing that God's uncharted way is the good way.

25
Faith and Witnesses
Hebrews 11:1-3; 12:1-3

Faith is the assurance of things hoped for, the conviction of things not seen.

Hebrews 11:1

WORDS FOR BIBLE TIMES

Christian history has often been a history of pain. To his followers Jesus said, "You will be delivered up even by parents and brothers and kinsmen and friends, and some of you they will put to death; you will be hated by all for my name's sake" (Luke 21:16-17). True to Jesus' words, the early church was destined to discover that the way to God's kingdom could be severe and terrible. The power and drama of New Testament faith was demonstrated through ordinary men and women who were filled with a spirit of commitment and bravery. History has shown that the Gospel message of hope has always been easier to understand by people under siege.

The passages for this lesson are small but important parts of a large section of the Book of Hebrews that deals with persevering in faith. The writer of the Book of Hebrews was apprehensive that some believers would not be able to stand fast during times of opposition, especially when threatened with bodily harm or death. Chronicles of the first century tell us of bitter reprisals and persecutions against Christians of all ages—in the arena, on the rack, facing the terror of savage beasts. So, the writer urges Christians to hold on, to endure hardships, and constantly to look to Jesus as their model and guide.

Hebrews 11:1-3 tells us that in order to endure, Christians must have real faith. And what is faith? Faith is the ability Christians find, through God's grace, to place more confidence in what God says about our situation than in what our enemies say about it. The enemy may say, "God doesn't hear you! God will not save you!" Faith responds, "God hears and cares. God is faithful." Faith like this becomes inner "assurance," a "conviction" that God can be trusted. With such faith Christians cannot be destroyed by the hardships of life. In fact, the writer states, each of the great heroes of Israel's past had this kind of absolute trust in God. (Read Hebrews 11:4-40.)

In Hebrews 12:1-3, the writer urges, in effect, "Don't become disheartened! When things look bad, remember the faith of our fathers and mothers." Therefore, we must run like trained athletes by (1) getting rid of anything that would slow us down, (2) not being distracted from the goal by sin, (3) keeping running at all costs, and (4) constantly looking to Jesus, especially when we are tired.

While others may be good examples of faith from time to time, Jesus is the "pioneer" and "perfecter" of faith. He has gone before us—through death and to God. His obedience and trust were perfect! In fact, he now sits at God's right hand of majesty.

WORDS FOR OUR TIME

In the early days of the church, the sincerity of a person's faith in Jesus Christ was tested quickly and harshly. To follow Jesus meant to quit following Jewish ritualistic practices, on the one hand, or to turn away from Greco-Roman religion, on the other. Such drastic decisions were met with misunderstanding, anger, and reprisal. So it is not surprising that by the third century the terms *Christian witness* and *martyr* meant the same thing.

It is difficult to imagine someone in modern America having to die for expressing faith in Christ. Yet people still do have to die for their faith—although most often in other parts of the world. On the whole, resistance to Christian witness in our country is more subtle. However, many Christians have experienced becoming family out-casts, being denied access to certain social groups, and even being lied about or falsely accused. For example, think of times you have been snubbed, laughed at, or in some way hurt because of your witness to Christ.

The writer of the Book of Hebrews urges us to remain steadfast in our faith regardless of the trials we face. Such a spirit of perseverance rests on three foundations.

First, we need to remember that the world is passing away. "You can't take it with you" is literally true! As important as life is, it is slipping away before our eyes. We need to be careful, therefore, not to invest ourselves excessively in what does not endure. The Book of Hebrews turns our attention toward the future.

Second, the only security we have is in God's promise of salvation. In Hebrews 11:3, the writer tries to illustrate this point. By faith, he says, we understand that the earth and the heavens are of divine origin. God "spoke" into existence what did not exist before. By the same token, faith assures us of the reality of God's kingdom; and so we live for it. Our faith rises above the limitations of our natural senses.

Third, convinced of God's presence and sincerity, Christians bear open witness to Christ in spite of any real or implied threat. Hidden in Hebrews 12:1-2 is a metaphor of a runner. The obstacles placed on the course are part of the race. Likewise, we should consider any obstacles we face as part of our course in life. Trusting Christ, we run to win against all odds.

How would your life change if you really viewed your obstacles as part of the race you are called to run?

WORDS FOR MY LIFE

In an athletic contest usually only one person rises to the top as the winner. In the Olympic games only one person is the fastest runner, the highest jumper, the strongest swimmer. The writer of Hebrews wants us to run the race of life with this kind of determination. The good news is that each of us can be the winner! If we live the

Christian life faithfully and patiently, we will win the prize. There is no reason for any of us to lose, because the Holy Spirit energizes us to make it across the finish line and into the winner's circle.

Fortunately, we do not have to rely on our own strength or skill to become the winners God wants us to be. Entering the Kingdom in no way depends on how intelligent or strong or gifted we are. What is important is faith in our God who saves. The writer of Hebrews tries to encourage us by telling us that "we are surrounded by so great a cloud of witnesses" (Hebrews 12:1). He does not mean that the witnesses of Hebrews 11:4-40 are sitting in some heavenly grandstand, cheering us on. Rather, it is the record of their lives of faith that becomes a source of strength for us. All these heroes and heroines of faith were ordinary people who lived lives of extraordinary faith because God was with them. They remind us that God will be with us too!

As important as the saints are, however, they are not the primary motivation for our Christian walk. Above all, we are called to look "to Jesus the pioneer and perfecter of our faith" (Hebrews 12:2). Jesus is our highest inspiration, not only because of what he did for us but also because of what he can still do in us. His determination to embrace God's will for his whole life becomes our model. Likewise, his strength to accomplish that will becomes our strength. With Christ in us and ahead of us, we cannot fail. If we "consider him," we will be able to resist growing weary or becoming fainthearted (Hebrews 12:3).

The host of faithful witnesses mentioned in Hebrews 11:4-40 lived a long time before Jesus. The writer of Hebrews did not realize it; but he was one of a new host of witnesses, along with the disciples and other New Testament Christians. Your church and mine is filled with contemporary witnesses who pray for us and encourage us. One day we will serve as witnesses for others. And to what will we give testimony? We will share the story of God's gracious work in our lives, as weak as they are. We will encourage others to look to Jesus, that is, to read of him, to learn from him, and to go to him.

26

The Church Triumphant in Heaven
Revelation 7:9-17

I looked, and behold, a great multitude which no man could number, from every nation, from all tribes and peoples and tongues, standing before the throne and before the Lamb, clothed in white robes, with palm branches in their hands, and crying out with a loud voice.

Revelation 7:9-10

WORDS FOR BIBLE TIMES

The Book of Revelation, with its strange language and mysterious images, uses its coded message carefully to unveil the destiny of the world and of the church, one to judgment and the other to the New Jerusalem. Originally written to encourage a persecuted church, its vital teaching continues to inspire confidence among Christians. The Revelation to John can become a book of worship and praise as God's final triumph over evil is surveyed, and the kingdom of God's glory is unveiled.

Our passage introduces us to a special group of people in heaven: the martyrs. These are persons who "have come out of the great tribulation; they have washed their robes and made them white in the blood of the Lamb" (Revelation 7:14). They were "slain for the word of God and for the witness they had borne" (Revelation 6:9). From the early days of the Christian movement to the fall of the Roman Empire, there were Christian men and women, boys and girls, who were brutally tortured and killed because they acclaimed Jesus as their king. Now the martyrs stand before God and receive God's reward for obedience and perseverance.

The martyrs wore white robes and held palm branches (symbols of victory and festal thanksgiving). Though they represented many languages and places, the martyrs praised God with a unified voice (Revelation 7:10). In this praise they joined the celestial beings in their adoration of the Almighty God (Revelation 7:11-12).

The martyrs now have a special function, to worship and serve God (Revelation 7:15). In return God protects, comforts, and nourishes them. The Lamb (Jesus) will be their eternal shepherd. As a reward for giving up their earthly life for the sake of the gospel, the martyrs receive "living water," the waters of eternal life (Revelation 7:17). These believers enjoy unbroken relationship with God.

Actually, the martyrs represent only one segment of Christ's triumphant church. Yet in the Book of Revelation they have a special role, doubtless because of the growing rejection and persecution the members of the early church experienced. Not everyone is called to witness to Christ through dying as a martyr. The church triumphant is composed of all who confess Jesus as Messiah and Lord (Revelation 14:12-13).

How does it make you feel to know that people have died as a result of their Christian faith? Why does God permit some people to suffer a martyr's death?

WORDS FOR OUR TIME

A student in one of my seminary classes wanted to make a request for prayer. Worry showed on his face. I told him to speak. What he said moved us deeply. "Pray for my mother. She has been terribly disillusioned [by a highly publicized sex scandal involving an internationally known evangelist]. She told me she no longer believes in God. She wants me to leave seminary. She said she would rather me be a member of the Mafia than a pastor." We all prayed. As far as I know, she never changed her mind.

This woman's reaction to the failure of a pastor was extreme, though perhaps not uncommon. She wanted a strong pastor, but he proved to be fragile. Her confidence had been shattered. Both the evangelist and the sincere woman point to a spiritual reality: The church is both strong and fragile.

The church is strong when it allows the power of the risen Christ to live through it. Jesus said that not even "the powers of death [can] prevail against" the church (Matthew 16:18). Christ has the greater power and shares that power with his people. At the same time, the church is fragile precisely because it is made up of human beings. The church can at times be all too human, but we must remember that Christians are people who have fears and anxieties like other persons. The beauty of Christian life is that God works in and through such "vessels of clay," making them fit for the Kingdom. We need to learn how to rely on the strength of Christ in the midst of human disappointments. At its best, the church provides an atmosphere in which we can do so.

Our passage shows that it is possible to bring fragile lives under the saving power of God. These triumphant martyrs were not superhuman. They were not free of distress and pain during their earthly lives. Each of them had his or her own story of fear, terror, and the grace of God. They were ordinary people who were given the grace to live extraordinary lives. These triumphant martyrs can become mirrors of our own possibilities in Christ.

Like any institution, the church can easily become power hungry, judgmental, and commercial. To be truly humble, serving, and forgiving is difficult. Yet the martyrs urge us to become such people. By giving us a glimpse of the future, the martyrs encourage us to become strong through Christ. The hope of the church is that the martyrs' glorious experience of the presence of God can become our experience too.

How should we act when Christians fail? How can we keep from failing? What do the martyrs teach us?

WORDS FOR MY LIFE

Standing in the presence of God, the great host of martyrs cried out, "Salvation belongs to our God who sits upon the throne, and to the Lamb!" (Revelation 7:10). Hearing this outpouring of gratitude and praise, the celestial beings joined in the mighty chorus: "Amen! Blessing and glory and wisdom and thanksgiving and honor and power and might be to our God for ever and ever! Amen" (Revelation 7:12). Can you begin to imagine this scene? Uncounted martyrs, unnumbered angels, and the throne of the living God and of the Lamb—such splendor, such joy!

By the grace of God, you and I will one day take our places in such a magnificent display of thanksgiving. We may not have been martyred like this majestic throng, but the overwhelming glory of the event will be no less meaningful for us. The theme of the martyrs will be our theme as well: Thanks be to God in whose hands the faithful are finally safe!

The figurative language of the Book of Revelation takes on an air of reality in describing this event in heaven. To illustrate the idea that nothing can really hurt those who trust in God, the writer puts words of praise in the mouths of those who have suffered the worst possible situation. What comfort this was to our sisters and brothers in the first century and what comfort it is to us. The vision of the redeemed in heaven is reassuring to Christians who suffer, whatever the reason.

A PERSONAL WORD TO THE READER

It is providential that the last lesson in this second volume of FAVORITE BIBLE PASSAGES should come from the last book of the New Testament. The passage speaks in a moving way of the triumphant joy of those who have fought the good fight, kept the faith, and at last behold the glory of the Lord. This is the Christian's eternal legacy through our Lord Jesus Christ. May it please the blessed God that you and I will one day participate in the reality of John's happy vision. Peace to you!

—J.L.M.

Meet the Writers

Brenda DeGraaf is Diaconal Minister of Education at Manchester United Methodist Church in Saint Louis, Missouri. In addition to her professional duties, she is homemaker, mother, choir director, piano teacher, writer, and baseball coach. She enjoys running, reading mystery stories, and teaching children how to sign for the hearing impaired.

Jerry L. Mercer is a frequent contributor to United Methodist curriculum resources. Dr. Mercer holds degrees from the University of Houston, Asbury Theological Seminary, Perkins School of Theology at Southern Methodist University, and the School of Theology at Claremont, California. At present Dr. Mercer is Professor of Preaching at Asbury Theological Seminary in Wilmore, Kentucky. He has also served as pastor of several United Methodist churches and as Professor of Religion at Azusa Pacific College in California.